His Promises For Me

Kathy Smoker

A Personal Account of Hope and Restoration

His Promises for Me

ISBN: 978-0-942507-09-6
ISBN: (E-BOOK) 978-0-942507-49-2

Address all personal correspondence to:

Kathy Smoker
828 Wallace Rd.
New Holland, 17557

Phone: 717-355-0150

Email: kathysmoker@frontiernet.net
Websites: www.kathysmoker.com / www.breakthroughGospel.com

Published by
Deeper Revelation Books
Revealing "the deep things of God" (1 Cor. 2:10)

P.O. Box 4260
Cleveland, TN 37320

Phone: 423-478-2843

Email: info@deeperrevelationbooks.org
Website: www.deeperrevelationbooks.org

Refer to website for an online catalog of all books published by Deeper Revelation Books, as well as distribution information.

Deeper Revelation Books assists Christian authors in publishing and distributing their books. Final responsibility for design, content, permissions, editorial accuracy, and doctrinal views, either expressed or implied, belongs to the author.

TABLE OF CONTENTS

Dedication

To my husband Benji. You are the love of my life. You have always ranked me higher, believed in me more, and loved me more deeply than I deserve.

Thank you.

Introduction

"For I know the plans I have for you," declares the Lord, "Plans to prosper you and not to harm you; Plans to give you hope, and a future" (Jeremiah 29:11 NIV).

God has a purpose for every person born into this world. He has arranged a beautiful plan of true happiness, joy, success, accomplishment and fulfillment for each person He has ever created. We are not here by chance or by accident. Rather, we are creations of the Most High God and are on this earth to accomplish great things for His Kingdom.

Even though we know that there is a perfect plan set in place with a good future in it for each one of us, we also know that there is an enemy roaming the earth. 1 Peter 5:8 warns us to *"Be sober, be vigilant; because your adversary, the devil, walks about like a roaring lion, seeking whom he may devour."* I believe there is a very real possibility of evil overtaking or short-circuiting the plans God has for our lives if we are not armed and prepared for battle.

Growing up, I was not equipped for spiritual battle. I felt the grip of darkness many times in my life, emotionally and physically. I didn't recognize the pain and confusion as being fiery darts from a spiritual enemy. Now, looking back, I thank

God that He pursued me and never deserted me. It seemed, time and time again, that there was an invisible barrier around me, something keeping me from stepping too far over the line. Now I understand that this invisible barrier was divine protection from the Lord, who was always there. Even in the most difficult moments, I know He was watching over me.

In the early years of marriage, as I started seriously seeking God's will for my life and studying the Bible more closely, I discovered that it contains many promises, from Genesis to Revelation. Making those promises personal, and claiming them for my future, opened up a whole new world to me. My eyes were opened to see that even though I had experienced a lot of pain and heartache in the early years, God had a good plan for the remainder of my life. Over time, through believing and receiving the good things He promised, I found myself being released from the bondage of chronic sickness, emotional and physical pain and wrong thinking.

I was born to Raymond and Sarah Smucker in June of 1972, the last child and much desired daughter in a loving family of five boys. I was joyfully welcomed into the family. My brothers were thrilled to finally have a little sister. I grew up in their shadows and loved the adventures of daily life on our spacious, rolling dairy farm, nestled into the valley of Churchtown, Pennsylvania.

All of the children in our family spent a lot of time outdoors on the farm. We worked hard and played hard too. Putting most of my energy into keeping up with my five older brothers, I hardly knew what housework was. But I could make my own fishing rods, fix broken tricycle wheels and help the boys assemble go-carts and other contraptions at an early age. I hold many fond memories of the fun-filled days, months and years we had on the farm.

Always ready for excitement, I loved being in the center of all the activity. My brothers and I enjoyed playing all the normal children's activities in our spare time—baseball, croquet, kick-the-can, four-square, hopscotch, etc.—and we spent hours every day roller-skating and riding our bikes all over the neighborhood. We also had a fearless fascination with danger, and were constantly pushing the boundaries of common sense and safety. I grew to love adventure and pursued it constantly. As a result, I had quite a few accidents, falls and close calls. It wasn't just a scratch here and a bruise there. It seemed I was getting hurt physically on every turn. In the most thrilling moments of adventure, something would go wrong and I wound up on the living room couch sobbing, with blood oozing or a limb that was broken. My accidents occasionally landed me in the hospital, nearly taking my life several times.

Over time, I developed a severe case of TMJ, a joint disorder in my jaw. Because of being jarred around so often, my jaw had gotten misaligned, knocked slightly out of place, and caused severe headaches and jaw discomfort. I tried to ignore the chronic and burning pain, and managed to push it to the back of my mind most of the time.

Sadly, there was a host of other things I was pushing to the back of my mind as well. In the midst of the frivolities of life that I enjoyed so much, there was an undercurrent of darkness that greatly affected me. I carried a deep, dark, haunting secret with me through the early years of my childhood. Like so many other children throughout the world, I was victimized by the perversion of sexual abuse at an early age. The fear that consumed me was real and menacing. I was terrified of being left alone. My bruised conscience slowly became hardened and void of much feeling at all. At an early age, I was experiencing psychological agony in my mind.

I also had a lot of muscular pain and tension in my body. The stress and constant fear due to the abuse magnified the problem in my jaw, causing me to grind my teeth at night while I slept, making the joint misalignment progressively worse. During the day, without realizing it, I constantly clenched my jaw. The grinding and clenching caused painful muscle spasms in my neck and shoulders.

The combination of emotional torment and physical pain became almost unbearable at times throughout my childhood and teen years. I was strong-willed and determined to enjoy life in spite of it, but occasionally the suffering rose higher than my tolerance level. In those times, buckling under the pressure, I retreated to my bedroom, collapsing onto my bed in misery. My tears soaked the pillows while tremors of pain riddled my body. I begged and pleaded with God to take away the soreness, the aching, and the awful tension in my muscles. When my prayers went unanswered, I consumed large amounts of pain medicine and narcotics until the tightness and discomfort was finally numbed and subsided. In those times I felt such dismal hopelessness. Feeling abandoned and alone, I silently wondered how my young life had gotten so difficult.

Unfortunately, I was well into adulthood and marriage before I could see how the physical pain in my body and the wounds in my spirit had numbed my thoughts and hardened my heart. On the surface, I had enjoyed a happy childhood. But at some point in my marriage, I realized that the betrayal and confusion in my past were still impacting my decision making, my attitudes, my sense of security and the way I looked at other people. By allowing the pain inside to control my thoughts and influence my actions, I was pulled into a web of destructive and harmful thinking and behavior.

A devoted, loving husband and other wonderful people who came into my life made me aware of God's redeeming grace and love. I found the power of His blood that is freely available to everyone, the blood of Jesus Christ that can cover all sin and restore every broken heart. I now understand the truths in His Word that can transform and make our lives new.

That is the reason for writing this book. I know with certainty that mankind has not been left alone and defenseless to face the evil in this world. No, we have a mighty, fierce weapon that will make the devil and all his legions tremble. God's Word is sharper than any two-edged sword, and the truths it contains are full of promise and hope for us today. Isaiah 55:10-11 unveils a great promise concerning the Word of God itself:

> *"For as the rain comes down, and the snow from heaven, and do not return there, but water the earth, and make it bring forth and bud, that it may give seed to the sower and bread to the eater; so shall My Word be that goes forth from My mouth: it shall not return to Me void, but it shall accomplish what I please, and it shall prosper in the thing for which I sent it."*

God says that He watches over His Word and is waiting to accomplish it. We can be assured that when we speak His promises into our lives, He will bring them to pass. Through the power and authority that's been given to us as joint heirs of Christ, we are able to take back the ground that's been lost, renew our strength, and rise up as on wings of eagles.

After I began applying these truths and claiming God's power in my life, I was astounded at the peace of mind and good things that began happening to me. A soft glow began to warm my heart. Like a healing balm, God's Word penetrated my wounded spirit, bringing me hope and restoration. Like a hungry lioness devouring her prey, I began to devour the Word of God.

I was excited to find hundreds of verses in the Bible that actually made a difference and worked powerfully in my life. I wanted to read them every day and memorize them, so I jotted down the verses that were most meaningful to me and placed them throughout our house. I found that writing or copying scriptures added a whole new dimension to my faith and understanding. Then I began to write Bible verses and quotations from Christian writers in notebooks, filling one notebook after another. After several years, a file in my filing cabinet was filled with Bible verses and messages of hope.

Recently, after clearing my refrigerator of the miscellaneous, multi-colored scraps of paper covered with edifying messages, I felt inspired to organize all my notes into a book. I wanted to share how these words of truth and promise have helped to transform my life.

When I had first entertained the idea of writing, I felt excited and enthusiastic about sharing the victories I'd experienced through God's Word. Then I came to the grim realization that it would also be necessary to revisit the battlegrounds. Victory never comes without a struggle, and a war is never won without a battle. I saw very quickly that it wouldn't be easy to revisit those experiences that had been the cause of so much anxiety. Furthermore my mind was bombarded with doubts, and I asked myself, "Why should I inscribe my story, which is merely a simple compilation of my life's experiences? Why would it be of any importance to share the path my wandering footsteps have trod, from early childhood through the tumultuous teen years, on into womanhood, to the person I am today?"

I also wrestled with conflicting thoughts about exposing the shameful things that were nicely hidden away out of sight in my closet of skeletons. I wasn't sure if I was comfortable with writing narrations from the secret chambers of my heart, and wasn't sure how people would receive them if I did. Nevertheless, after battling this thing in my mind for a few months, I decided to go through with writing my story in its entirety with boldness, letting the chips fall where they may. I felt I must write it for many reasons. There is an entire world 'out there' that is filled with pain and violence because of abuse and its drastic aftermath. I wrote my story for the little girls and boys in the world who are suffering, at the mercy of people with malicious, sick and selfish intents. I wrote it for the parents who are looking the other way, either intentionally or just because of a lack of awareness. I wrote it in hopes of raising that awareness and giving children the protection they deserve. I also wrote my story for adults who have simply 'outgrown' a troubled or disturbed childhood, but are still stuck in the pain and dysfunction it has brought.

I know there is hope and healing after abuse, whether it is sexual, physical or verbal. Because of this, I am confident in the purpose and power that my personal account holds. My faltering steps have taken me from a pit of darkness into the light of the greatest love known to mankind. My journey has brought me to the heart of the most important person who ever lived. That person is my Maker, the Savior of the world, Jesus Christ. So this book is not merely about my life. It is about the One who rescued me from a life of destruction, giving me hope for the future and the deepest peace I've ever known.

As I dug into my deepest recollections, I was forced to search my soul. I had to take a painful journey into the past and relive moments and days that had long been put to rest. I felt as if I were on an emotional roller coaster, sometimes laughing and other times crying. Many times, my heart and mind felt as if they were tied in knots, as old memories and feelings reawakened within my body and spirit.

It is my prayer that through reading about my trials and frustrations and the scripture verses that helped set the score straight in my life, you will be able to use them to do the same in your life. I know now that God was waiting for me to turn to Him, waiting to answer my cries for help. He was always near, waiting to pull me back to Him. But I had to take the first step. I had to ask for His help. Then I had to follow through and walk in the plan He has for me.

We only get one chance to live. I hope that everyone who reads my story will begin to honestly come to terms with any hurtful memories from the past. There is restorative power available to everyone who will seek and ask. I want to help you make use of that power, and take back the good things the enemy has stolen. If we speak truth into our lives, we have a promise that we will not be drawn away when we are tempted and tried. All believers will be confronted with the temptation to doubt God and His Word. Even Jesus was tempted by the devil in this way. To overcome, we must confidently respond the same way Jesus did in His hour of temptation. He answered with the written Word: (Matthew 4:1-11) *"It is written."*

In the last section of this book, I have included a catalogue of my favorite Bible verses, arranged according to subject. These verses are strong words of truth, and they hold the power to change lives forever. Claim them as your own, and let God's promises become real for you.

I hope and pray that you will be blessed and that your life will be renewed because of my story. It is a story that began with scraps of paper containing great promises from the Word of God. These promises have helped me, and I know that they will encourage you to proclaim truth and victory for your life and the lives of your children and loved ones.

With love, *Kathy*

SECTION ONE

Bittersweet Beginnings

You have taken account of my wanderings;
put my tears in Your bottle.
Are they not in Your book?
(Psalms 56:8 NASB)

CHAPTER 1

Innocence Lost

I loved playing in the farm buildings behind our house, in the old tobacco shed, the corn crib and especially up in the hay mow where all the rabbit and guinea pig cages were. I spent many happy hours in the damp, musty confines of the buildings, exploring and playing imaginary games. There were endless things to discover in those old spaces, and they pulled me in like a magnet.

As a little girl with an independent spirit, I loved to roam. Many times, my wandering footsteps carried me into the large haymow, upstairs in the barn. It was a quiet place, a peaceful haven of mystery and delight. Within its cool, stone walls was where I loved to be.

All of a sudden, the mysterious lure of farm treasures and the sweet smell of baby bunnies mingled with a tightening, sick feeling in my little tummy. I knew from previous times that danger could be lurking in the shadows. I tried to block the memories, but they kept filling my mind. I could faintly hear one of the neighbors shouting in the distance. I knew he must be working outside, tinkering with one of his old cars. It wasn't my neighbor who struck terror within me. It was his teen-aged son. He spent most of his time alone, roaming the neighborhood. I only hoped and prayed he wouldn't come looking for me today.

An uneasy feeling deep inside warned me that I had better return to the safety of the house where Mom would be cheerfully baking pies, doing the weekly cleaning or washing the family's clothes in the basement. But I decided to play a little while longer. Oh, how adorable the cute, furry, soft bunnies were. I laughed aloud in delight while watching the babies scurry and hop around in their straw-lined pens.

Suddenly, fear gripped my heart as I caught a glimpse of movement, a shadow moving silently toward me in the darkness of the barn. I felt his eyes on me. I knew he was watching and waiting to snatch me away. Frantically searching the walls surrounding me for a way of escape, my eyes rested on the beam of light shining through a crack in the old barn door. My heart was pounding so loudly. I felt if I ran fast enough I could escape into the warmth of the sunlight outside, just ten or fifteen feet away. In an instant, his tall, swaggering form came out of the darkness, and he was beside me. He gripped both of my tiny arms in his strong hands, dragging, pulling my small, wriggling body across the barn floor. Realizing I was no match for his strength, I became subdued and quiet, as utter hopelessness flooded over me.

In the dark corners and shadows of the barn, embarrassment and shame overwhelmed my tender spirit. My body trembled as his hands caressed me. Everything inside me was resisting his grasp as he pulled me into his lap and cradled me in his arms. "Don't be afraid," he whispered, over and over. Feeling vulnerable and exposed, I lay rigid, avoiding his gaze. My eyes darted to the barn rafters high above. I watched a lone pigeon as it flitted from one rafter to another. My heart echoed its mournful coos as it gently flapped its wings, making the eerie silence of the barn more bearable. Trying to escape the inner turmoil I felt, I closed my mind to the confusion within.

I felt some of the tension begin to release, and my body relaxed as I gave in to my captor's desires. Knowing that his probing, intruding questions commanded a "Yes," I dumbly nodded my head in agreement to everything he asked. My mind was filled with questions that had no answers. "Why is this happening to me?" I wondered. "Why do people do things like this to little girls?"

Although he had told me many times that all children do these things, I couldn't make sense of it. But I was beginning to believe it, no longer doubting him. The strong, feisty spirit I had been born with was becoming weak and wounded, numbed by the confusion in my mind.

When his cravings were satisfied, he released me. Deep inside the walls and canyons of my soul, I was no longer an innocent child. I was a prisoner, a captive to the spirit of fear. I had no idea then that this fear would follow and torment me for more than twenty years. As a child, I did not know that it would nearly destroy me. The fear was so strong and became such a part of me that I could not imagine living without it.

Sexual abuse, especially at such an early age, had a disastrous effect on my young, innocent mind. There was a point when I came to accept the abuse as being normal. I can almost remember the day when my thinking changed. Not being able to remember how or when the abuse started, the fear and confusion simply became a part of my daily life and routine. I came to fully believe that every child endured this type of crude behavior, no longer doubting the lies my abuser used to control me.

Occasionally, I was able to spot him as he approached, allowing me to escape to the safety of the house. But my escapes only taught my tormentor to be more cunning and devious. He learned to creep up stealthily behind me, suddenly jumping out of the shadows, gripping my arms tightly in his strong grasp. Not knowing anyone was near, the adrenaline and terror that coursed through my body at those times was surreal. At times, I felt suffocated as my heart pounded wildly inside my chest. My attacker stifled my screams by quickly slapping his hand over my mouth, and my cries for help went unheard.

In my mind, this was the worst type of fear imaginable. I became extremely anxious and nervous. The fear I felt was intense and unrelenting. Most of my thoughts were consumed with avoiding its source. My wanderings on the farm were no longer carefree. Now everything centered on the distress that was taking over my young life. No matter where I played, I listened for his footsteps. I was constantly on edge—looking over my shoulder, jumping in alarm at the slightest sound. I could not enjoy playing in the barns anymore, and being alone in those old buildings made my skin crawl.

Helping my older brothers with the milking and feeding on most evenings, I spent many happy hours by their side in the cow stables. But after the milking activities were over, I had a choice to make. I could either wait for my brothers while they washed the milkers in the milk house, or I could make a lone dash for the house in the darkness outside. The thought of trying to run for safety filled me with dread. So, most of the time, I waited impatiently, bored and restless, sitting idly by while my brothers got everything ready for the next milking in the morning. Sighing with relief as they finally finished their nightly task,

I could then leisurely walk to the house by their side, enjoying their light conversation and the cool night air.

Occasionally, I just could not tolerate the boredom of waiting for my brothers to clean the milking machines, and I mustered up enough courage to run to the house alone. Running as fast as I could, I dashed through the darkness, the terror within me rising with each pounding step. Glancing behind me as I ran, I felt sure that someone was waiting in the shadows, waiting to reach out and grab me. This drove me to run faster, and it was with relief that I reached the porch steps. Taking one giant leap to the top of the steps, onto the porch, my spine still tingled.

A devastating, paralyzing sense of panic became my constant companion. Every area of our large farm was now tainted with the spirit of fear that followed me. Many times, I went against my better judgment and went back to the barns. My love for animals lured me into the cow stables and hay mows time and time again. I lost track of time while following a mother cat to her new litter of kittens or trying to catch another glimpse of a spunky, new calf that had just been born. It was easy to become completely engrossed in the sweetness and breathtaking newness of all those farm babies that I loved. My voice could be heard sweetly singing or speaking to them as I admired their markings, and held them close. In those moments, my wounded heart became soft and tender, and I found great comfort.

All thoughts of tenderness quickly vanished when, time and time again, my abuser crept out of the shadows, and I realized I had been trapped once more. I knew it was too late to escape when I heard his footsteps coming closer and felt his hands on me.

The house where we lived was a refuge, a place of safety where nothing bad ever happened. I tried to find comfort within its walls. But even the corners of the rambling, stone farmhouse in which we lived brought anxiety to my heart. The only places I really felt safe were in the large, open kitchen and the adjoining living room where we spent many happy times together as a family. All of us loved to play games or gather around the old, brown gas stove. We laughed and talked, passing the long evenings.

When bedtime came, I dreaded leaving the safety and warmth of the kitchen to climb the long flight of stairs to my room. My bedroom was large and spacious, a dream come true for most little girls. For me, however, the room held terror and nightmares. The three windows in the room tormented me; I always felt as if someone was watching me through them. The fear of being watched day and night grew into a kind of phobia. I believed that someone was always following me, even in my own home. I begged and pleaded to sleep downstairs, away from those big windows, away from the darkness.

My family seemed baffled by my extreme behavior, and they often asked me what was causing my fears. Mom bent the rules for me many times, allowing me to sleep on the couch in the living room. Even there, troubling dreams frequently awakened me. I lay awake battling the mounting fear in my mind until I thought I would surely go crazy. Shuddering violently, I buried myself deeper into the covers, trying to shut out the pictures in my mind.

I developed a very strange habit that became ingrained in me and continued for years. Whenever I felt threatened or afraid, or felt like someone might be following me, I quickly put my hand behind my back, palm facing outward. In my mind, the act of holding my hand behind my back in this way put a barrier between my body and whatever I felt threatened by. For a reason I can't explain, this lessened the fear, made me feel safer, and gave me a sense of control.

The most difficult part of it all was being alone in my pain. "It's our secret," he always told me when he released me. "No one can know what we do." I felt I had no choice except to hide the fear. Whenever I found enough courage to mention my fears, I was bombarded with questions: "Why are you so afraid? What are you afraid of?" With my abuser's voice always in my head, I clammed up and pushed my fears deeper inside. But I knew exactly why I was afraid. My fear of one man eventually expanded to a mistrust of all men.

My childlike mind remained in a state of war. I examined people from a distance, trying to see inside their souls, trying to decipher whether they were good or bad. I labored over how to tell which adults I could trust and which ones were not trustworthy. How could I tell the difference? These thoughts tormented me.

Any adult male, except my brothers and my dad, had to earn my trust. Otherwise, I would not even smile at him. The years that should have been the most carefree and trusting years of my life were clouded with mistrust and worry. I exhausted my mind and my heart trying to regain some kind of control over my life.

My friendships with other children became the brightest spot in my life. The happiest memories in my childhood are of being surrounded by many friends. I felt empowered in that realm, and greatly enjoyed being the ring-leader and the life of the party.

The neighborhood, one-room school I attended was a wonderful place for me. It was a place of safety, fun and camaraderie, where everyone could be trusted. Fortunately for me, every teacher I had from grades one through eight were women who were gentle, sweet and kind. Every moment there was pleasurable, and it was one of the few places where my guard could be let down completely. The only problem I had in school was getting into trouble with the teachers occasionally. I loved my teachers, even adored a few of them. I know they loved me as well, but they couldn't always tolerate my acts of mischief.

There were about thirty students in our school, and we had grades one through eight in a one-room schoolhouse. The lower grades, one through fourth, sat on one side of the room in rows of desks, and the upper grades, fifth through eighth were seated on the other side of the room. To prevent confusion and keep order in a room with so many different grades, we were expected to be reasonably quiet as we concentrated on our lessons, with very little interaction. The only people moving about or talking were usually the classes that the teacher was in session with at the time.

Always being a social butterfly around children my age, this became a bit stifling and boring for me. Whispering and passing notes to other students was normal behavior for me, and I did lots of it. The boys in school liked teasing my girlfriends and me, so we had constant 'battles' and joking going on, mostly taking place during school hours. The teachers kept a close watch on us, but even so, whoever sat behind me was usually harassing me regularly. I was always prepared for anything from having sharp pencil tips jabbed into my shoulder blades to someone placing upturned tacks on my seat. I thrived on the attention and the boys anticipated the serious pay-back they knew would come later.

Special occasions at school were the highlights of each term for me. Whether it was days we went on field trips or the day of our school's year-end picnic, I would wait impatiently for the planned date to come weeks before its arrival. Our school had a Christmas program every December. The programs were interesting and festive, offering many poetry recitals, plays and humorous skits by the students. I'd always had a special love for poetry, as long as I can remember; so I was delighted in that first year of school, when I was asked to recite a poem at the Christmas program.

On the day of the program, I could hardly wait for my turn to come, and when it did I eagerly took my place in the center of the stage, facing everyone's parents and siblings, including mine. The crowded schoolroom became so quiet you could have heard a pin drop. I stepped forward and breathlessly recited my short poem in the community's favorite language, Pennsylvania Dutch. It was a charming little piece, and funny too. When finished, I stood basking in the thunderous, roaring applause and laughter that erupted! It was my first experience with performing, and I relished the moment, enjoying it greatly.

The most uncomfortable situation I encountered at school was when I was in sixth grade, and the teacher asked me and four other students to stay after school one day. For a reason that I can't explain, we had all carved our initials into our desktops earlier that day. At the time it seemed harmless enough, but later, alone in the schoolroom with four other guilty students and one disgruntled teacher, the air was thick. We were given a long lecture about being disrespectful and destructive of property which didn't belong to us. She went on and on. I lowered my head, glancing miserably at the beautiful initials that were now causing such problems for me. However, I couldn't help smugly thinking how nice they looked. After her speech finally came to a close, our teacher descended upon us, ruler in hand. "Hold your hands out, palms down," she barked, and proceeded to whack each person's hands with the sharp edge of the ruler. The strikes were sudden and sharp on my knuckles. I had always wondered what that would feel like, and decided it wasn't as bad as I thought it would be; but I couldn't remember ever being so happy to walk through those schoolhouse doors and head home as I was that day.

I liked to make the other kids in school laugh, and would've done almost anything to be humorous. One day, a few of us decided to chew gum during school hours—which we weren't allowed to do—just to see how long we could get away with it. About a half-hour into session, the teacher noticed me chewing, and promptly asked me to spit my gum into the trash. The waste can sat in the front center of the room beside the teacher's desk. With all thirty students curiously watching, I marched up the aisle, shoulders squared, head held high. Pushing the gum to the front of my mouth with my tongue, I leaned forward over the trash-can and dramatically thrust the wad out of my mouth at a high rate of speed, making a loud hissing noise. To my delight—and everyone else's—the waste can was completely empty, and the wad of gum hit the bottom with a resounding "ping." Everyone snickered and laughed. Grinning, I returned to my seat, mission accomplished. Surprisingly, the teacher just rolled her eyes, trying not to grin, and resumed classes.

Although the social life was the main source of enjoyment in school for me, learning always came easy for me and I really did enjoy that part of it too. I felt safer and more relaxed in school than at home. Because of that, the classrooms, the playgrounds, and everything surrounding school called to me, pulling me in. After eighth grade was completed, I begged my parents to allow me to continue on through high school. But in the culture we grew up in, high school was not considered necessary. The tears flowed as I rode home from school on my bike on that last day. I couldn't imagine never going back to school again, and felt very sad.

My abuser found many ways to convince me that what he did to me was normal, further distorting my view of all humans, especially men. He used vulgar, coarse language when he talked to me, and I grew accustomed to hearing an array of despicable words that most respectable adults will not use with each other. As a little girl, I knew and understood the meaning of his vocabulary all too well.

He also put a whole host of questions in my mind about the animals on the farm, such as the day he found me gazing adoringly at a litter of sweet-smelling, new puppies. I loved baby puppies more than anything in the world and delighted in how precious they were as they gently nuzzled their mother. Being so tiny, they still didn't have their eyes open. I enjoyed watching them climb over each other, while squeaking softly. My abuser settled in beside me, his breath warm on my neck. He spoke softly, "See, even the puppies are doing it." Then, leaning closer, his hand moving up my back, he whispered into my ear, "All babies do it."

I was shocked as I absorbed this awful news. My hands trembled as I tenderly stroked the puppies' soft, tiny bodies. "No, no, it can't be true!" I thought. These puppies were so adorable and sweet. They were too small and too pure. I didn't want to believe what I was hearing. And a part of me didn't believe it. But my heart was breaking because another part of me did believe what he said. I could never look at the puppies after that without those thoughts going through my mind.

Eventually, as I grew older and stronger, I began to fight my abuser and was no longer putty in his hands. While tagging along with Dad and the boys in the barn one evening, I was happily helping with the feeding, chattering loudly to my older brothers while watching them heave shovels full of chop into the cow's feeding troughs. I enjoyed this tremendously. When the feeding was done, I quickly tired of watching the remainder of the milking process. I had become bored with this part of the procedure.

After several silent arguments with myself, I decided it would surely be harmless to venture upstairs into the hay mow to play with the bunnies while my brothers were so close by. Creeping up the ladder as quietly as a mouse, I walked over to the cages. Breathing a happy sigh of relief, I whispered, "There you are, my furry little friends. I've missed you." As my fingers traced the wire surrounding their cages, my eyes watched their carefree, bouncing movements. I smiled as they wiggled their little pink noses.

Suddenly I stiffened, hearing the sound of shuffling footsteps in the straw. I turned and fled, but not fast enough. His hand gripped my arm, twisting my body around to face his. I opened my mouth to scream, but his free hand quickly muffled my cries. I felt myself being pulled away, the usual sinking feelings of hopelessness overtaking me. Glancing backward, I could see the light shining from a single light bulb covered with cobwebs and dust. The comforting glow of the light slowly disappeared into the darkness and shadows of the far end of the hay mow, a place I never ventured into alone.

The feelings of claustrophobia were closing in, and my spirit revolted against the things I knew he would do to me. I hated the way his hands invaded my body, as he spoke the lies that were penetrating and influencing my mind. I could feel his desperation to keep me under the shroud of deception and confusion that had ensnared me. I could sense the very real presence of something awful and menacing that was there. I could smell the breath of evil all around me. I could feel the depth of it and taste the bitterness of it. My young spirit, once pure, was inhaling the destructive vapor, and it was consuming me.

I had long before realized my own frailty in the face of his towering strength and knew how futile it was to struggle or try to run. But this time was different. Somewhere deep within, I made a silent decision, a determination that would bring about a defining moment in my life. Fury shot through my whole being, and a strength that I didn't know I possessed came over me. I fought with every ounce of muscle my small body contained; wriggling, kicking, scratching, and squirming, not giving up until I felt his grip loosen.

To my surprise, I felt myself break free! With tears blinding my eyes, and frightened sobs escaping in sharp, painful gasps, I ran. I plunged through the darkness as I fled, stumbling over clumps of hay and uneven boards in the hay mow's floor. In a surreal haze of blindness, I could hear the sound of my blue canvas sneakers pounding loudly on the wooden floor, but my feet felt nothing. My body was numb and void of any feeling at all. It felt as if I were floating.

As I clambered down the ladder to safety, I heard his mocking, taunting voice from above, "Go run to Daddy! Run. Run!" Then, like the blow of a sledgehammer, I felt the full weight of his next words, "Remember, don't tell anyone." I can clearly remember the impact of that moment, as I heard, absorbed, and fully responded to those familiar words,

At the bottom of the ladder, I leaned weakly against the wall, hiding in the shadows, needing some time to stop crying. It was hard to breathe normally. The light from the cow stable shone through the window to the dimly lit feeding area. I could hear my brothers talking and laughing as they finished the last of the milking, but I knew I must not tell. "It is our secret...no one can ever know."

I didn't understand how the power of those words, "Don't tell anyone!" could be so strong. Why did that threat work so well with a child? Why does that threat work with almost any child? I submitted completely to that command, never thinking it through, but just accepting it as a command from someone I must obey. I look back and see how the awfulness of the secrecy held me spellbound. I grappled with the mystery surrounding those three words.

I finally gathered enough courage to tell my mother about the fear, shame and pain I was enduring. I don't remember how old I was when I finally defied his authority, and revealed our secret. I have reasons to believe it may have been between my fifth and seventh birthdays. Nor can I remember what brought on my confession. It could have very well been the courage I gained after physically breaking free and fleeing to safety that night. Something within my spirit continued telling me this wasn't how things were supposed to be.

I felt great relief when my mother said, "This victimization is indeed unacceptable and should not continue." However, I was much less satisfied with her solution to the problem. She said, "Run to me, and stay close when the neighbor comes over. I will protect you, and keep you from being alone with him." My immediate reaction was great relief, and I felt comforted and protected.

But it wasn't long until my anxiety level was doubled, if not tripled. I soon discovered that keeping track of my extremely busy mother at all hours of the day could be exhausting. Fearfully, I tried to play while keeping Mom within eyesight and earshot at all times. She flitted all over the large farm, in the basement doing wash one minute and at the end of the lane mowing grass the next minute. It seemed impossible to know where she was every minute of the day, and eventually I just gave up and stopped trying to stay near her.

I went about my days trying to play and have fun, sticking close by my brothers when possible. I grimly decided to make the best of my situation and take care of myself as well as I could. My abuser continued being a frequent visitor to our farm, coming and going as he pleased.

Trying to restore the carefree attitude I once had as a young child, I attempted to live a normal, happy life. The years passed by, but the fear continued to follow me, plaguing my mind, and clouding my thoughts. My phobias only seemed to worsen as time went on, and I struggled with these negative feelings daily.

I loved spending long summer days outside on the farm, but the second I saw him walking in the lane, I quickly ran in search of Mom. When I could not find her right away, I became panic stricken as I dashed through the house, the basement, and the garage. I searched in the vegetable garden and in the orchard. A few minutes seemed like an eternity to me. Upon finding my mother, I would resign myself to follow her wherever she went, no matter how bored I became. Many times, I watched sadly from the house as my abuser and my brothers spent hours shooting birds from the big maple trees with their BB-guns. I would have loved to be outside as well, but to stay safe I confined myself to the house. Although not bound, chained, or locked behind closed doors, I was a prisoner.

In my childlike reasoning, it felt as if my parents cared more about my abuser's feelings than mine. He freely walked all around our property while I was fearfully glued to my mother's side. He was even occasionally welcomed into the house, where I watched my family laugh and talk with him as if he were a good friend. This sent a clear message to me that the harm he did to me really was not worthy of a confrontation. As I beheld my family's open acceptance toward the person who had violated my body, spirit, and soul, I felt abandoned and betrayed. Then there was another larger part of me that wondered if I was overreacting or being immature and babyish. I berated myself for being so sensitive. In vain, I tried to push the questions and nagging thoughts out of my mind. I tried not to care so much. Nothing made sense to me anymore.

My parents' reaction to my situation was not lining up with my overwrought emotions, so I decided there must be something terribly wrong with me. After all, I was just the baby of the family. Surely my parents knew best. Therefore, I told myself, "They must be right, and my feelings must be wrong." I didn't realize that my parents couldn't possibly understand my situation clearly, with the minimal information I'd given them. Instead of telling mom the whole truth of the things my abuser did to me, I was embarrassed and held back details, only giving scattered tidbits of what I was enduring. I showed little emotion, hid the deep fear, and covered my pain. I didn't realize how crucial it was that I tell her everything!

After several short and very sparse conversations with Mom concerning my plight, the subject was dropped. My parents never spoke to me about my fears until many years later, after I was well into adulthood. They didn't know the extent of my misery, nor did they have any experience with the subject of sexual abuse or the damage it does. I was left with a heavy load of emotional baggage to carry alone, and felt the full weight of its burden every day.

As I matured and grew, there were times when I tried to sort through the details surrounding the abuse and find reasons for the doubts and questions in my mind. I tried to rationalize the terrible fear that seemed to follow me everywhere. Not being able to find the answers, I tried to convince myself that my disrupted childhood had been normal and acceptable. It was confusing to me. In so many ways those years growing up on the farm had been wonderful and good, definitely overflowing with love, and filled with excitement and fun times, but everything was tainted with a sense of alarm and uncertainty.

Along with the unanswered questions and troubling thoughts, my mind was also filled with warm memories of being surrounded by a close-knit family who I always knew loved me very much. I remembered sitting next to my mother at church and the wonderful smell of her perfume. Many times she would coax my head onto her lap and lovingly rub my ear while the preacher's voice droned on. I remembered the frequent thunder showers we got every summer. Fascinated with the sharp cracks of thunder and piercing darts of lightning, I would sit by the window in the old farmhouse to watch the storm, but it was never long before I felt Mom's arms around me, coaxing me away from the window. I knew she would stay close to me until the storm passed. I wasn't scared, but always welcomed her protection anyway. I remembered our family kneeling every morning and listening to Dad praying from the worn and tattered prayer book. I loved the comforting sound of his gentle voice and the presence of God's Spirit, but for me the best part of our family devotions came after it was all over. Dad always picked me up and carried me to the kitchen, laughing and joking all the way. This was a special time of bonding every morning that I loved and looked forward to.

Because of ignorance and lack of awareness, my parents failed to protect me when I needed protection the most, but in every other way, Mom and Dad were very loving and attentive parents. We spent quality time working and playing together as a family. When I felt safe I couldn't have been happier. Because of this, I learned to block out the bad times, and simply learned to live for the good times. I developed a driving hunger for fun and excitement. Seeking out the thrills and highs in life helped to numb the pain I was experiencing; but still I wondered why I struggled so much emotionally. Ashamed and embarrassed because of my deep fears and sensitivity, I desperately tried to be tough and strong, suppressing and hiding those negative feelings. Looking back, I don't know which was worse, the fear or the deception in my mind. Both had drastic effects on my childhood that carried over into my teen years. I felt incapable of discerning right from wrong in many situations. My conscience, although extremely sensitive in some ways, became dulled and numbed in others.

As a girl budding into womanhood, I hated the turmoil I felt. I wanted to be stronger, and longed for the ability to stand on my own. Holding onto all of my good intentions, I promised myself things would get better. I convinced myself my situation was not so bad, and everything would be alright.

CHAPTER 2

First Encounters with God

I have learned that all of our yesterdays shape our tomorrows. Every experience, each encounter—the happenings of our past—have brought us to where we are today. I have also come to believe that whether we like it or not, our past experiences will always affect us, to some extent.

While it is not good to live in the past and dwell on old hurts, I have realized the importance of accepting the things that lie behind us for what they are. Denying that bad things ever happened is not the path that leads to healing. Blocking out parts of our past will never bring the closure needed to move on to the great things that God has for us. However, facing and conquering the shameful and humiliating events of our past can bring emotional wholeness and strength, allowing us to be true overcomers.

I don't understand why some people enjoy sweet memories of a past filled with safety and love, while others carry heavy burdens of heartache and pain throughout most of their lives. But I know that God is faithful and will walk with us through every trial and difficulty if we ask Him to do so. I love the promise in Isaiah 43:2 that says, *"When you pass through the waters, I will be with you; and through the rivers, they shall not overflow you. When you walk through the fire, you shall not be burned, nor shall the flame scorch you."*

As I look back over my life, I can say that I've been richly blessed. I was blessed to be born into a warm, loving Christian family, blessed to be married to the man I love and blessed to be the mother of four healthy, beautiful daughters. I am so thankful for my own family today and for a wonderful husband who protects and cherishes me.

At the same time, it took many years to recover from the great heartache I suffered. As a child, my life was darkened by fear, mistrust and confusion. I believed that life would always be bittersweet, that the joyous times would be laced with misunderstandings, secrets, and feelings of inadequacy. The earliest years of my life became a potpourri of good and evil; and in a strange sort of way, they were so intertwined I could hardly separate the two.

We grew up in the shelter of a Christian family that attended church and Sunday School. My brothers and I were taught the plan of salvation from the early days of childhood. My parents were both born and baptized as Old Order Amish church members. After they married, my parents began attending an Amish Mennonite Church where things such as telephones, electricity and automobiles were accepted. Even though a much more modern lifestyle was embraced, the dress code stayed similar to the Old Order Amish way with the use of head coverings and homemade clothing.

My mother dearly loved and missed the Old Order Amish lifestyle. She missed the simpler way of living, and she became more and more discontent with the more modern path which she and Dad had chosen. This subject came up repeatedly, and became a huge source of discord in our home. My dad was farming a large farm and dealing cattle on the side. He enjoyed having the luxury of driving his own cattle trucks and using tractors and machinery equipment to do the field work. Neither of those luxuries were allowed in the Old Order Amish church, so he was closed to the idea of returning to the church he grew up in.

Finally, after several years of disagreements, bickering and heartaches, the decision was made to reach a compromise. Our family would join the New Order Amish church, where automobiles were not allowed, but we would still be able to use telephones, electricity and farm machinery. I was seven years old when we made the change. This was all new to us children and we were fascinated with the new turn of events!

The following week, Dad sold his cattle truck, pickup truck and car, trading them in for a shiny new black and grey buggy. Along with the buggy, he bought a strong and fast retired race horse. We were most likely the family who traveled to and from church with the most speed every Sunday. Dad was impatient with fancy show horses and just wanted to get from point A to point B as quickly as possible. I was proud of him and his choices of horses, and enjoyed our swift travel mode thoroughly.

Instead of going to a church house to worship, each family took turns holding the church service in their homes, so we attended church at a different place every Sunday. Before our first time going to the new church, I went with Mom to an Amish store where she and I were both fitted for stiff, hard black bonnets which we wore over top of our white coverings. Next she bought me a black shawl, which I would wrap tightly around my homemade black coat during the cold winter months. The boys and Dad's dress code didn't change much, but our dress and cape patterns needed to be made in a plainer and less fancy way, so Mom was busy sewing for a few weeks.

We settled into the slightly different lifestyle with ease. I didn't mind the change. It wasn't a whole lot different from where we'd come from, just a few minor things. Making new friends came easily and effortlessly to me, and I quickly struck up close and rewarding friendships with all the children that were my age. It didn't matter to me where we attended church, because I truly enjoyed growing up in the plain setting and adapted to any changes that were required, easily and without questions.

We continued being a faithful part of the New Order Amish Church for the next seven years, but later, when I was fourteen years old, Dad made the firm decision to return to the Amish Mennonite Church. Mom agreed to it, and she did find true happiness there. My parents never argued about the subject again.

So that was that, a seven year bubble in our lives that didn't really make anything better or worse for me. I had a good time wherever I was—as long as I felt safe—so I never had a church preference, or gave any of it much thought. The change was interesting and I enjoyed it for the most part. To me it was simple. I enjoyed the great Bible stories and didn't care where I learned about them. I eagerly memorized many of the beautiful accounts of the miracles of Jesus, tucking them away in my heart.

Although my young mind had been tainted with uninvited filth, my heart was still pure. I always desired to have a greater understanding of the Word of God and wanted to know more and more.

My mother's dream was to have eleven sons and two daughters. She managed to get almost half-way there with five sons and one daughter. My brothers brought much pleasure and fun into my shadowed childhood days. Their constant bantering, pranks and mischief were a welcomed distraction to the internal conflicts I faced. The best word to describe the whole pack of them is "fun-loving." There was never a dull moment on the farm, and we had an over-abundance of good belly laughs in our home.

The lazy days of summer brought simple pleasures such as swinging high on a tire swing under the old maple tree in the front lawn or better yet, dangling from a rope swing hanging from the high rafters in the hay loft. My brothers and I fought about whose turn it was to swing and struggled to hold on when two or three of us rode the swing at the same time. We also spent a lot of time down by the meadow playing in the creek, building dams, sliding on mud slides, swimming, and fishing with homemade fishing rods. It was a wonderful place to cool off and we had hours and hours of fun there; but the highlight of each summer came on the days when we were allowed to bike over to a nearby pond to swim the warm afternoons away. Ringler's pond was open to the public and sat in the middle of a meadow along a quiet country road at the bottom of the long lane leading up to the Ringler farm. Families from all over the neighborhood would walk or ride bikes to and from the pond. Happy and excited children of all ages would eagerly approach the cool waters while their mothers or older sisters unpacked picnic baskets full of freshly made sandwiches, snacks and homemade desserts. It was a fun place to be, and many summer days and occasional evenings were passed away there in simple bliss with friends and family.

The long winter months held the excitement of snow sports and neighborhood parties. Everyone we knew owned a newly sharpened pair of ice slates and a good sled. Skating on the neighboring ponds and creeks, or sledding on the rolling surrounding hills, were two of the main winter activities. After daily farm chores were finished, we enjoyed skating away long evenings on the winding, frozen creek in the meadow. The creek flowed on for miles, and on the days it was frozen hard enough, we skated to school and back home again, filling our lungs with cold country air. The best skating, however, was on our cousin's nearby pond. My brothers and I were often welcomed into Aunt Rachel's kitchen afterward, to warm up before the cold trek home. There we swapped stories with our cousins, told jokes and had lots of laughs while devouring warm and sticky caramel corn, hot chocolate and whatever else might have been prepared earlier for the tired and hungry crew of youngsters.

When the ice was too soft to skate on, or after a fresh snowfall, the sleds came out; most of the older siblings joined the younger children riding homemade sleds under the stars at night. Occasionally we tied three or four toboggans together and hooked the lead sled to a horse; then we all piled on and went skimming across the open fields. A fine frosting of snow and ice covered our huddled forms, and the night air stung our cheeks!

On the farm I loved to help feed and milk the cows and even raised a few of my own calves. I always had a deep love for animals, and showered my affections on the many kittens born on the farm. I was gifted in taming the wild, hissing kittens, sitting close to them for hours, silently luring them to me. Knowing that the kittens would tame quickly as soon as I held them and scratched their little heads behind the ears, I took the challenge often. I loved it.

When Dad taught me to drive the skid loader and the big John Deere® tractors, I was thrilled to be able to help my brothers in the fields. I can still smell the sweet fragrance of new hay as the machines formed bales and thrust them onto the hay wagon behind the baler. Waiting there, my brothers stacked the bales on the wagon to later put into the hay mow.

When it came time to harvest the corn and fill the silos in the fall, my excitement peaked. I loved to be in the center of all the farm activity and stayed outside every evening until Mom sent me off to bed. Pleasant thoughts of the evening's exciting activities flashed through my mind as I fell asleep to the rumbling sound of tractors pulling wagons full of silage past the house.

For the first five years of my life, I thought I was a boy, and I spent the next eight years wishing I were just one of the boys. Oh, how I admired my brothers and tried to be just like them. To my mom's great distress, I even tried to walk like the boys, taking large, halting steps in my pretty dresses. Then, when my brothers reached the age where swearing was the cool thing to do I picked up the lingo quickly, and all sorts of interesting new words came out of my mouth. The fights my brothers and I had were rough-and-tumble brawls. I learned at an early age to defend myself well. I freely scratched, clawed, walloped, and yelled, whatever was necessary. But my brothers didn't seem to care much, rarely correcting me.

My siblings and I grew up in harmony that was only occasionally disrupted. To my great delight, the boys included me in some of their mischief and pranks. One day, they all gathered around me, laughing loudly as they cut off big chunks of my long, brown hair. I felt honored to be such an important subject of interest at the moment, although I did not feel as happy later when Mom saw my hair.

I must say that when push came to shove, my brothers defended me, and I like to think that they would have protected me with their lives, if they had been called upon to do so. My brothers were always extremely important figures in my life. Each big brother adored me and spoiled me beyond words, becoming more protective as the years went by.

I spent most of my time with John, who is only eighteen months older than me. He told me all sorts of tall tales, always pretending to know the facts about everything even when he didn't have the slightest clue of what he was talking about. I idolized him and believed every word he said, but still we argued incessantly. Mom laughingly tells us how she could hear us yelling at each other all the way to the creek to go fishing, and she wondered how on earth we ever caught any fish with all that noise! But we did catch lots of fish, tadpoles and frogs, built dams together and made big plans to build bridges—which never actually came into being. We were best friends and he watched out for me. When I was asked to stay after school because of mischief I'd gotten into, John was the one who waited under the bridge down the road for me, because he knew if I came home later than he did, I would be questioned and punished for getting into trouble at school.

Andrew was three years older than me and spent a lot of time with John and me; but it seemed he was never sure who was most interesting—John and me, or his three older brothers. He drifted back and forth between the older set and the younger set of children in our family, and sometimes got lost in the shuffle. He was very sensitive and kind. It was restful spending time with Andy and if I needed someone to talk to, I knew he'd be a good one to seek out.

It was the older boys, Lester, Dave, and Sam, who got stuck with taking care of me a lot. During my first school year, Mom thought I was too small to ride my bike the two and a half mile distance to school; so I was precariously plopped onto the seat of one of the older boys' bikes, and they transported me to and from school every day of that whole year. My five brothers and I usually met up with an even larger crowd of neighbor boys on their bikes and we all rode the remainder of the way to school together, taking up the whole road sometimes. The boys seemed to forget I existed while they talked and laughed loudly with their friends. Being juggled from side to side on a very uncomfortable, narrow bike seat for a total of five miles every day doesn't sound like much fun, but I loved it. Listening to a bunch of big-headed teenage boys bragging and telling wild, exaggerated tales—along with a little bit of truth—was entertaining, to say the least. With the wind blowing through my hair and a grin on my face, I hung on tightly to the swaying hip of whoever was burdened with my forty extra pounds that day. I also hung onto every word that was said and learned an awful lot that year.

While my brothers lovingly watched out for their little sister, they thoroughly enjoyed teasing me as well, and seemed to do so with every opportunity given them. One summer Dad gave the older boys permission to buy three large white geese and bring them home to the farm. To my great distress, the geese were extremely aggressive and I quickly became their favorite person to harass. I don't know if it was my brightly colored dresses or the piercing screams that erupted from my mouth whenever they were around, but something about me highly excited those geese. There wasn't much that my brothers enjoyed doing more than opening the gate and releasing the three honking bullies just as I was riding by on my little purple bike. Without fail, all three geese immediately went into overdrive, screeching after me, wings flapping noisily and beaks wide open, snapping and groping at my legs while the boys roared in laughter.

It was hard to believe that the same boys that laughed so uproariously when I was terrified could be so concerned and protective when I really did get hurt! However, they got plenty of chances to show sympathy toward me in the years we spent on the farm.

The long string of mishaps I was involved in all seemed to start at three years of age when my brothers and I were upstairs in the haymow one morning; the boys were busy working and I was playing nearby. Following Dad's instructions, my brothers were shoveling and pushing a large pile of loose straw down the "hay-hole" to the floor level of the barn, where they would later use it for bedding in the cow's stalls. I was absently listening to their casual chatter as they quickly got the job done. They instantly grabbed my full attention however, when one after the other, they jumped through the hay-hole into the pile of straw below, and immediately climbed up the ladder to do it again. I was at my brother's sides in a second, hanging onto their arms, begging them to "help" me jump too! They didn't give it a second thought, and picking me up off my feet, they happily took turns swinging me through the hole onto the quickly disintegrating pile of straw. We had hours of fun and it seemed harmless enough.

The next morning, remembering the thrilling time we'd had the previous day, I wandered up into the haymow alone and jumped through the hole again. Of course, my brothers had finished their job of spreading the pile of straw into the stalls nearly twenty-four hours earlier, and I landed with a loud thud on the cement floor. Thankfully my brother, Andy, and my dad were working in the barn, and heard the fall. I was rushed to the hospital where I spent the next five days being carefully monitored and nursed back to health.

I continued being accident-prone; at five years of age, I broke a bone in my right leg while jumping from the kitchen table. When I was seven years old, I fell from my bicycle and rolled directly in front of a concrete truck, helplessly watching the front wheel of the 60,000 lb. vehicle come to a screeching halt, just inches away from my head. A little while later I fell from a wagon load of hay, tumbling over and over on the stone driveway. I still have scars on both knees to show for it. A speedy thrill-ride on a homemade go-cart we built (with no brakes) landed me in the roadside ditch scraped, bruised and bleeding. The go-cart was busted so bad we couldn't use it anymore. Somehow I got thrown off my bike on the way to school one cold winter morning, and sure enough, wound up in the doctor's office again—this time with a concussion and a throbbing, swollen, black eye. Another time, lying on the dirt ground after falling from the ladder going to the haymow, I slowly and gingerly moved my body, terrified that something was broken or bleeding; I sighed with relief to find that every bone was still intact and I had survived with a mere bump on my head, a few bruises and a pounding headache.

I managed to stay in one piece, and for the most part the misfortunes I encountered weren't too serious, just annoying and usually painful. However, I guess it was bound to happen sooner or later; on a rainy and dreary Sunday afternoon when I was eleven years old, I had a severe accident. My cousins, brothers and I were playing upstairs in the barn at my older brother Lester's farm. In the midst of an exciting game of Broom-Sock, I was fleeing a determined pursuer who was close to catching me. Laughing loudly, I jumped onto a bale of hay that, unknown to me was covering a hole normally used for throwing hay to the cows in the stable below. Down I went, through the hay-hole, for the second time in my short life. The bale of hay and I landed on the cement floor ten feet below.

Everything went black, and I woke up several minutes later to the anxious faces of my cousins and brothers. No one said anything. They all just looked down at me with terror on their faces. My head and my ear throbbed. I lay helpless on the cement floor, while one of my brothers used the phone hanging on the barn wall to call Mom and Dad.

My parents immediately rushed to the farm where I lay waiting for help. Mom's face was filled with fear as she tenderly picked me up and carried me out of the barn. I was carefully transported to our home where Mom fretted, worried and cried—frantically doing everything she could to make me feel better. This was back in the day when parents did not rush to the emergency room for every accident in the family. Evening came and I was resting peacefully. In spite of Mom's pleadings, Dad made the decision to wait until morning to determine if I actually needed to see a physician: "If she has a concussion, then we will take her to see a doctor."

My mother endured a dreadful and worrisome night sitting by my side, praying continuously. She sensed something was terribly wrong, because I couldn't maintain my balance when I tried to stand or walk. Throughout the night, I vomited blood and spoke incoherently. I was delirious, and cried out repeatedly in my sleep. After watching me hallucinate from the pain and seeing how sick I was, Dad realized that my injuries were serious, and I was taken to the doctor's office. Our family physician was concerned, and recommended that my parents admit me to the hospital immediately for further testing. Once there, CAT-scans revealed a blood clot that was resting on my brain. Nurses began shaving the right side of my head in preparation for emergency surgery. I don't think I will ever forget the minutes just before surgery when I was alone with Mom. The surgeon, aware of the seriousness and dangers of this type of operation had warned my parents that there was a chance I would not survive. Mom knew she needed to have a very difficult conversation with me, her only daughter. Sadly, she asked me, "Kathy, if you don't pull through the surgery, would you be ready to die?"

I took a few seconds and thought seriously about her question. With no apprehension, I replied, "Of course, Mom. I would go be with Jesus." I didn't give it another thought and had total peace as I went into surgery. As always, I was curious, checking out my new surroundings in the operating room. Regardless of the pain, I watched with great interest and amazement as two nurses shaved off most of my hair.

I woke up hours later and soon grew accustomed to the white, bandaged head I saw in the mirror. I didn't cry until a few days later when the bandages came off and I saw the ugly staples. I had no hair on one side, and my ear stuck out two inches. I cried and cried, thinking about my friends' reactions at school and at church. "I will be so embarrassed," I said; "Everybody will stare at me."

And stare they did. I thought I would hate all the curiosity and the questions about how I lost half of my hair, but I ended up enjoying all the attention! Everyone catered to me in the weeks that followed, and I received all kinds of special treatment from my brothers, parents and friends. I absolutely loved the gifts, cards, scrapbooks and candy that people brought when they visited me.

The fall from the hay mow was my first close encounter with death. When I thought about meeting Jesus face to face at the age of eleven, it didn't strike fear in my heart. I actually felt happiness instead. I knew that Jesus really loved me, and this love made me feel secure and protected.

At age eleven, I was sure that Jesus loved me, but my faith in His love faded as I grew older. The hidden sins that trashed and littered my childhood days and teen years slowly chipped away at my certainty that I was cherished by my Maker. It often seemed to me that the evil in the presence of my abuser had won the battle for my heart and soul. Looking back, the best word I can use to explain how I felt is "numb." I did not have much of a conscience, so I flirted with disaster without considering any of the consequences. Physically or spiritually, life did not hold much value for me.

As changes took place within my body, my dad constantly urged me to become a young woman of grace. Stubbornly, I clung to my boyish ways and habits. Acting ladylike bored me, and I carried a wild restlessness within my spirit. My inner spirit, although once tender and soft, became more hardened as the years slowly passed. By the time I reached my teen years, I didn't feel as if I could possibly overcome the many strongholds that had gripped me over the years. I could barely remember the sweet, shy, sensitive little girl I once was. My mind was consumed with fun, friends and excitement; and I would go to great lengths to get what I wanted, no matter what the cost.

I knew in my heart that some of the things I was tempted with weren't acceptable. I even knew that most of my temptations were actually gross sins in the eyes of God. With every year that passed, I felt more guilt and conviction, but I could not seem to find the inner strength or desire needed to change my behavior. At the age of fifteen, however, I realized that I was immature and unfulfilled. I felt empty inside. I desired to become the young woman that my father so desperately wanted me to be. I wanted to change my life and my attitude, and resolved to make a fresh start.

I felt very good about my decision to join Instruction Classes at church. This was a pleasant time when teenagers met frequently with our congregation's ministers to study the Bible and learn more about the ways of a Christian life. We knew the plan of salvation, having been taught about Jesus' death and resurrection as small children; but in the classes, we went over the details of the familiar story again. We also discussed what it means to have a personal relationship with Jesus. Furthermore, we were reminded of the importance of keeping and living up to the church's standards, along with the reasons those standards had been put in place to begin with. There were certain requirements needed to become a member of the church, and we covered all of them in depth. After the required period of instruction and teaching, the ministers deemed us ready to be baptized and receive membership into the church.

I enjoyed this special time of spiritual growth, and especially looked forward to the time our class spent interacting with the ministers. For whatever reason, I'd always had an extreme fascination and admiration for anyone who preached God's Word. Evangelistic speakers particularly fascinated me. During these instruction classes, I remembered being spellbound at revival meetings when I was a child. I would feel totally lifted out of this world. I eagerly drank in every word of the anointed speakers.

I will always remember Aiden Troyer, a fiery preacher and traveling evangelist who proclaimed God's Word with great passion. His sermons shook me to the core of my soul. I remember wanting to go forward for prayer when he extended the invitation, but I knew little girls my age were not allowed to do that. Sitting next to Mom in the tightly packed church house, I lowered my face to hide the tears stinging my eyes. Not knowing why I was crying, I only knew that my emotions overflowed and my heart ached under Rev. Troyer's sermons. I wanted him to pray for me, but didn't know why. Many times I have wondered how my life might have taken a different turn had I found the opportunity to ask that great man of God all of the unanswered questions that were swimming in my young mind.

The time spent with the pastors of our church during instruction classes was interesting and stimulating. I was hungry for approval and eagerly sought to prove my worth to my teachers, trying hard to please them. I felt the void in my heart being filled as I turned to God. I could sense His Presence and felt my relationship with Him deepening. I wanted to experience more of His power in my life and vowed to live for Him, with a pure and free heart.

When asked to bring my favorite Bible verse to the final meeting of the classes, I searched the Scriptures, trying to decide which verse truly meant the most to me. I couldn't seem to find one that really spoke to me until I read the words in Psalms 27:1: *"The Lord is my light and my salvation; whom shall I fear? The Lord is the strength of my life; of whom shall I be afraid?"* It spoke loudly to my spirit, calming the deep fears I still carried within. Over the years, I quoted it often and still treasure those words today.

On the day of my baptism, I waited expectantly as the water dripped down onto my lap. The pastor spoke the words over me, "Kathy, in the name of the Father, the Son, and the Holy Ghost, I baptize you." I desperately wanted to feel God's overpowering presence, to hear His voice, or to experience a mighty rushing wind...something, anything.

I felt a small tinge of hope stirring within my mind, but I was disappointed to still feel the usual numbness. I did not feel the power and excitement that I expected, but I knew that baptism is an outward symbol of my commitment to God, a celebration of a new beginning. I was secure in my faith that promised Christ's inner joy would come to me at some point, so I felt a sense of importance and value. I did feel closer to Him, and knowing the love of Jesus in my heart was comforting to me.

CHAPTER 3

Accompanying Sin

After we turned sixteen, my friends and I began attending the youth group activities at our church. This should have been a great time in my life. For a short while, I enjoyed meeting with the small youth group, and the fellowship that was there. The Bible studies we had with the youth leaders intrigued me. Studying the Word created a hunger for a deeper connection with God. However, I felt restless, and couldn't seem to be satisfied. I could not seem to truly find or experience the meaningful relationship with God that I so desired. At times, I could not feel God's power in my life at all. Although I longed for His protection and authority, there seemed to be an obstacle looming large and menacing between my Maker and me.

In the months that followed, my girlfriends and I became bored with the small youth group, tiring of doing the same things every weekend with the same few people. Feeling dissatisfied with life, we finally made the decision to look for ways to have fun elsewhere. It didn't take us long to find other connections. Unfortunately it was with a group of kids who were deeply involved in partying, drugs and immorality. My friends and I felt that we were strong enough to hang out with a crowd that indulged in sin without succumbing to the immorality around us. We developed quick friendships and felt at ease with this new crowd.

We remained friends for several months without giving in to the sin all around us. We stood firm in our convictions and did not yield. We justified ourselves by thinking we were being a light and a Christian example to these new friends. Of course, we didn't mention anything about this new crowd of friends to our parents. However, over time they found out about the reputations of our friends, and our associations became a church issue.

The ministers came to pay me a visit, warning me of the dangers in this indulgent lifestyle, urging me to discontinue any friendships that violated the teachings of the church. They asked me to cut all ties with this rebellious group of teenagers. Sitting in the living room on a hard chair with four somber ministers facing me was very intimidating. It was so unlike the pleasant times we had together just a short while before during Instruction classes. My heart pounded as I looked miserably into their eyes and took in the warnings and advice they were offering. They gently told me the road I was on would eventually lead to hell. They were concerned, and the words were spoken in love, but in that moment something awful took hold of me and shook me to the core. The fear and frustrations that had been churning within my spirit for years seemed to be magnified one hundred times over. A hot, burning mix of anger and terror rose up like a roaring fire inside of me.

Satisfied that their duty had been fulfilled, each of the ministers shook my hand and filed out, departing with a few last words of encouragement. I bolted from my chair before Mom or Dad could get started with me, and fled up the carpeted stairs to my private place of refuge. Slamming my bedroom door loudly, I flung myself across my bed. I don't remember how long I lay there thrashing and screaming into my pillow, pounding the mattress until I was exhausted. Sobbing, I finally fell into a deep and troubled slumber filled with disturbing dreams of darkness and flames devouring me.

The sun rose again the next morning as if nothing had happened. I went through that day and the days following in a haze of confusion and sadness, wondering what the future held for me. I wondered if my salvation was being snatched away, little by little, and if I would be doomed to eternal torment, even though I was crying out to God daily. I wondered if anyone cared at all about the internal pain I was carrying and had been carrying for years. I wondered why no one ever asked how I felt inside, or what I was thinking about.

I desperately wanted to be "good," but there was a yearning in me for excitement, a passion that was driving me. I just couldn't tolerate the feelings of boredom and emptiness I felt when there was not something exciting happening. Inside I felt nothing; nothing but emptiness. My heart had closed in a long time before, becoming tough and hardened to the outside world. Furthermore, I couldn't feel God's presence in my life, or His love, for that matter. Over the next few weeks, I made my decision. No matter how much the ministers of the church warned me, I felt I could not turn away from the one thing I thought would fulfill my desires.

The thing that had the strongest hold on me and drew me into the party scene was the music. My girlfriends and I became close friends with a group of guys who played in a rock band. I had always loved music, so I was completely fascinated with the band, and all of their instruments. They got together every weekend to practice. My friends and I loved to watch them practice on the weekends. We loved the pounding rhythm of the drums and the loud music. I spent as much time as possible at the practice hut.

Knowing how passionate I was about music, the guys in the band would occasionally humor me by giving me the spotlight behind the keyboard with a microphone. They strummed along while I belted out a few of my favorite country songs. It wasn't their cigarettes, alcohol, lewd conversation or behavior that pulled me into the group. I really loved the music. When anybody mentioned going to the band's practice hut, I automatically let down my defenses.

Not giving any heed to the pastor's warnings, I continued spending time at the band's hangout. I enjoyed its dimly lit walls, the loud music and the endless card games. Through a haze of cigarette smoke that was constantly swirling upward into the air, I looked on for hours as the band worked together, trying to perfect every song they knew.

As time went on, I began compromising. It became easier to say, "Yes," when I knew I should say, "No." Temptation came from every direction, and my resistance to it was becoming weaker and weaker. I was plagued with boredom if I was not with my new friends, but when I was hanging out with the band, I felt pressure to give in to the temptations.

My parents became suspicious of my activities, always questioning me when I left the house. I grew weary of their hovering over me, feeling smothered and confined. I tried to avoid their prying eyes and close scrutiny as much as possible. Eventually, I openly defied them: "Leave me alone; I am capable of making my own decisions."

My parents and I drifted apart emotionally and stopped communicating. The atmosphere at home was tense, and my once loving relationship with Dad became strained. I could always argue with Mom, and we could get it out of our systems. Dad was a different story. As I rebelled, we grew further and further apart. I felt condemned because he was appalled at what I was becoming. Our conversations got ugly, and I talked back smartly, and was rude. I took my anger and negative feelings out on Dad.

I knew the disrespect toward my father was very hurtful. I felt bad, especially when I thought about the good old days when I had followed him all over the farm, constantly being in his shadow. My heart ached when I remembered the many trips he and I took in his cattle truck to the New Holland Sales Stables. Then I was a little girl, sitting proudly next to her father on the old, dark blue seat that gently creaked and swayed. I loved those trips when we happily talked and laughed together.

My heart swelled with pride when Dad's burly farm friends affectionately called out to me, "Hey, Smucker!" Everyone knew with one glance that I was his daughter, because we looked so much alike. The ultimate highlight of the day came when Dad asked me to raise my hand to bid on a cow or calf he was interested in buying. I felt very important as his smile of approval beamed down on me. After the cow sale was over, he always slipped a quarter into my hand to spend on the gumball machine.

In those days, Dad was my friend and my hero. I felt safe and protected when I was with him. I greatly admired him as only a daughter can admire a father. Even the simple act of watching him wash his hands after a hard day's work on the farm was fascinating to me. Standing on tiptoe to lean over the sink, I watched in amazement as he took the green bar of soap in the wash bowl to lather his hands and arms. I never tired of seeing the clean, cool water from the faucet wash off the dirt and grease.

In my memories of the good times with Dad, I smiled to myself as I mused over a heartfelt conversation we had on a warm summer day in my early childhood. In a rush of love and affection, I said, "Dad, when I grow up, I want to be just like you."

Grinning, he asked, "Oh, and why might that be?"

With conviction and certainty, I solemnly replied, "Because you always take one day at a time." I couldn't understand why he laughed so much at my answer, so I just shrugged my shoulders and laughed too.

Now, all those pleasantries seemed a long way off, and these days were anything but pleasant. The tension between us rose up more and more with each passing day. I no longer wanted my father's attention and spent as little time with him as possible. I wanted him to stop worrying about me, quit trying to control my every move, and leave me to myself for a change. After all, I was seventeen years old already!

Sermons at church no longer held my attention. I found myself gazing out the window during services, mentally making plans for the rest of the day. I often passed notes and giggled with my girlfriends, not hearing a word of the sermons. Then the rumors started circulating, some true and some false. The church decided to take disciplinary action against my friends and me, and we had a few awkward meetings with the ministers. We were asked to make public confessions at church, which was followed by excommunication from the church family. They told us, "We are putting you on a six-week proving period. If, at the end of that time, you repent and remove all sin from your lives, we will take you back into full membership."

By this time, my father and I were barely acknowledging each other, and the few words we exchanged were cold and tense. I could feel his disappointment in me, and he felt my growing animosity toward him. The pain and misunderstandings were great, and the wall rising between us seemed insurmountable.

CHAPTER 4

One Step Forward-Two Steps Back

My next year was filled with rebellion and heartache. It wasn't bitterness or hatred for things of God that drove me to disobey my parents and the church. Quite the opposite: I loved the people in the church, loved my parents and felt an awe and respect for God.

What drove me to disobedience was the utter boredom and emptiness I felt in my spirit. It would have been great to stay within the safety and shelter of a large group of Christian friends, and I longed for that. However, our youth group dwindled down to a few faithful members, and the ones who were there could not seem to find common ground or make any real connections.

Throughout my eighteenth year, I was only somewhat successful at keeping my feet grounded in the safety and familiarity of the church. The discontentment I felt on the long weekends was building, and I drifted further and further into a world that I wasn't prepared to handle.

My girlfriends and I lived lives of secrets, half-truths and deceptions as we struggled to maintain our new friendships and relationships while trying to stay in the good graces of the church. The months passed in a blur of confrontations and confessions; the judgments that rained down on us were many. Although the church had taken us back into the fellowship as full members, within a few months, I found myself standing before the congregation once again, forced to make yet another public confession. Baring the secrets I had been carrying, I felt remorse and shame. The ministers and the congregation excommunicated my friends and me for the second time.

Our lives became very public, and it seemed everyone was talking about our rebellion. I felt the curious stares as we filed into church on Sunday. At first, I felt shame. But as time went on, I ignored their questioning eyes and developed an "I-don't-care" attitude, hardening myself to other people's opinions and condemnations.

The new relationships I so eagerly threw myself into had their own problems and disappointments. I was unprepared for and appalled by the lawlessness, lack of conviction and utter ungodliness that I had embraced. I wondered how people could be so hard, so rebellious and so calloused. It bothered me that my new friends did not seem to care about God, eternity or their own salvation.

I tried to make sense of the situations I had gotten myself into. I had let down my guard so many times that I could no longer see where I was heading. Things took a turn for the worse in my life when I allowed myself to be pulled into more serious relationships with some of the guys I knew. Trusting and vulnerable, I didn't realize how unprotected I really was out there on my own. On a very dark night that will always be etched into my memory, I trusted the wrong person. Not seeing it coming, I once again found myself trapped, held against my will, and taken by silent force. The shocking reality of what was happening somehow couldn't reach my brain; and like I'd always done with everything else, I made light of it. Telling myself it wasn't a big deal, I refused to admit I'd put myself in a bad situation and gotten hurt because of it. Outwardly, I laughed about it, shrugging the whole thing off; but inwardly my heart ached with indescribable confusion and turmoil.

The next few weeks were a miserable existence for me. This time I was completely silent in my distress, not uttering a word of what I was enduring to anyone. I was sick with regret, worry and remorse, and wished I could go back in time. I wished for a second chance to take the advice given to me when I had been warned of the many dangers lurking in the world. My spirit became weak and lifeless.

Three days after the victimization, I was running some errands in Reading, Pennsylvania, about thirty minutes from where we lived. As I drove through an unfamiliar town, I was deep in thought. I felt lost in the world of misery I had built up for myself, and turned the very recent happenings over and over in my mind, shutting out the world around me. Tears threatened to tumble from my eyes, but I remained strong, bravely holding them at bay.

Suddenly seeing the road I was looking for, I absent-mindedly made a left-hand turn, and pulled over directly into an oncoming vehicle. The man driving the pickup truck was going full-speed, and didn't have a chance to slow down. The crash was loud and the impact of it projected my body forward into the windshield, shattering the glass into small pieces that rained down on me. As my forehead hit the windshield, my teeth came down on my tongue. Fortunately, the sudden and fierce bite didn't slice it off completely; my swollen, bleeding tongue was still held together by a small sliver of skin. My knees were sliced open as they were shoved into the dashboard. Then, as if it wasn't bad enough already, I felt a sudden impact from behind and heard the grating crunch of another car hitting the back of mine. My body was forcefully slammed back into the seat, giving me severe whiplash. I blacked out and came to a few minutes later inside a screaming ambulance, where the nurses were cutting off my homemade dress and apron while the driver of the ambulance rushed me to the closest hospital.

Within a couple weeks, the bandage that had been carefully wrapped around my head came off, the stitches in my forehead were removed, the eight stitches in my tongue came out, and my knees were scabbed over. On the outside, I looked like I was healing just fine, and all appeared to be well; but on the inside, I was broken in pieces, wounded and hurting.

It was during this period of time that I had a life-changing experience during a meeting with one of the pastors, Ben Smoker. This man later became my father-in-law. I can't remember if I called him or if he called me. In any case, we scheduled a meeting at his home on a warm, clear summer evening.

My emotions were tied in knots, because most of my talks with ministers in recent months had not been pleasant. Anxiously, I knocked on the door. Ben greeted me with a welcoming smile and suggested we sit outside, "It's more pleasant under the tree at the picnic table," he said. As we sat down, I tried to calm the pounding of my heart, dreading yet another difficult conversation. I knew that the ministers all meant well, but the meetings I'd had with the other pastors had seemed pointless and held no real meaning for me.

Placing his focus on me, Ben gently said, "I know you're going through a difficult time." Unwanted tears immediately welled up in my eyes, overflowing and slipping silently down my cheeks. I lowered my head and nodded, unable to speak. Then he proceeded to talk, slowly and kindly. He seemed to realize how difficult it would be for me to speak through my tears, so he talked instead. I was relieved to sit and listen, gathering my composure while he told me stories about personal experiences in his early life.

He had known some of the same feelings I was experiencing now, feelings of restlessness and searching for more, not knowing how or where to find it. He shared with me how he had discovered the pathway leading to God's great love, even while being rejected by the people around him. Examining the cracks, splinters and chipped paint on the old picnic table, I listened intently as he spoke in his gentle tone, without a trace of bitterness or anger. His whole being radiated a spirit of peace and contentment, something I deeply desired.

When my gaze finally met his, I was surprised to see compassion in his eyes, as if he really cared about me. The walls that I had so carefully built up slowly started coming down. Hope filled my hungry soul, and the questions poured out of me like water. Ben patiently answered each of my questions with confidence and truth, never condemning me or being harsh.

I will always cherish that evening. The cold, bitter wind that was blowing across my heart warmed in the sunlight of love that evening from someone I least expected.

He never realized it, and I wish I had told him before he passed away how the time spent with him on that warm summer evening made a permanent change in my spirit. I went through the rockiest period of my teen years shortly after I met with Ben. During that difficult time, the kindness and encouragement I received from him was not forgotten. Remembering his words of truth and love softened my heart many times, and I was never quite the same after that.

I will always remember that evening. I will always remember a gentle, old preacher's stories of hope in the face of disappointment and misunderstandings. I will always remember the softness and compassion in Ben's eyes as he spoke, and I will always remember how good it felt to know that there was someone who still believed in me. Someday when I meet him again, I hope to tell him, "Thank you."

I made a deliberate and conscious effort to separate myself from the temptations that had plagued me throughout my teenage years. I even told my dearest and most beloved girlfriends that I would not be hanging out with them on a regular basis anymore. The next few months were bittersweet. Though I didn't join in with any questionable activity, I sometimes offered to be my friends' chauffeur, dropping them off at their destinations and picking them up later. I tried desperately to find positive ways to fill the emptiness I felt inside, knowing that I had to separate myself from the temptations that previously had such a strong hold on me.

I missed the time with my friends terribly, but consoled myself with a newfound sense of peace. I could not describe my new serenity as true "peace." It was more an absence of guilt, but that was enough. I no longer had a burning, searing conscience bothering me. That felt good and was sufficient for the time being. After being taken back into full membership again at church, I vowed not to mess things up again.

I was restored to fellowship with the church, but I felt so alone. Struggling daily with the feelings of boredom I'd come to hate so much, I just couldn't continue turning down the constant invitations from my friends. Without fully committing to them, still trying to be firm in my resolve, I occasionally went out for an evening or just a few hours, thinking it would be harmless.

What followed was a very difficult time in my life. I felt torn and pulled in two directions. The hunger for companionship and friendship was great, and it seemed that my hunger could only be satisfied in the company of the only real friends I knew. But the constant parties and frivolity no longer enticed me, no longer aroused my senses or attracted me. Instead, I felt heavily convicted, and my sensitivity only seemed to heighten as time went on. I longed for a life that was more substantial, holding meaning and value.

Eventually, after entering into a dating relationship, I found it easier to cut all ties with my close girlfriends, the ones who knew my deepest thoughts, the ones with whom I had shared every area of my life. I purposed within myself to seriously pursue a life of purity and godliness, no matter what the cost. That was what my heart desired.

Throughout the next year I sought comfort in the string of dating relationships that followed. Hungry for love and affection, I opened my heart time and time again, only to end up feeling trapped and suffocated a few months later. As each new relationship deepened, I felt my identity being snatched away, little by little. I couldn't stay true to who I was or stand for what I believed. As I reluctantly surrendered more and more ground to other people's wishes, it felt like a noose was tightening around my neck, closing in around me, snuffing out what little energy was left in my spirit. I became emotionally spastic, and felt completely incapable of returning the love that was offered to me. It seemed the more I was sought after and pursued, the more I felt confined and manipulated—and the more heartless I became. Each dating experience ended abruptly within a few weeks or months.

I felt completely lost and alone during this time. The darkness that had gripped my soul and the aching in my heart was hard to describe in words; but that was not a problem, because I had no one to talk to anyway. There was very little communication with my parents; my brothers were cold and distant; my girlfriends were no longer in my life, and my position in the church was rocky and unstable, as always. I had few real friends—for the first time in my life—and constantly felt stuck in relationships I didn't want to be in. Somehow, my life had become a nightmare of confusion. Losing all touch with reality, I felt incapable of making my own decisions, and my sense of self-worth and value was plunging to a dangerous level. Futilely sorting through my thoughts and emotions, I cried out to God over and over again, praying that He would rescue me and bring fulfillment, true happiness and peace to my soul. I could not find what I was searching for and never felt settled.

The peer pressure and the insecurities I experienced within the unfamiliar boundaries of new relationships made me feel extremely vulnerable. Becoming increasingly unhappy, I allowed myself to be pulled into areas of sin and darkness that I hadn't been exposed to before. I felt foolish when my conscience scorched my heart time and time again, heavily convicting me. I realized how sheltered I had been compared to the people I was now associated with. I hated being so sensitive and felt ashamed and immature. Telling myself to grow up, I willed myself to let go of my petty ideals and hardened my heart once more.

The restless spirit stirring within was now driving me, pushing me to recklessly abandon better judgment, urging me to go against everything I had ever been taught. I wanted to live my own life.

CHAPTER 5

My Mother and I

One Monday morning, Mom and I were gloomily driving together to her craft shop in Morgantown. After a long weekend of worrying and fretting, not knowing where I'd been, Mom reached her breaking point with me, angrily muttering, "If you're planning to live like this, and want to put me through all this worry, you may as well move out."

Without hesitation, I quickly replied, "Fine, I will."

We drove the rest of the way in stormy silence. I knew well enough that she did not mean it. I knew it was just her way of saying that as long as I lived at home I needed to abide by my parents' rules. One part of me wanted to be obedient and live a good life, but I felt so confined, so smothered by the very people who had given me life.

Without Mom's knowledge, I was busy making arrangements to mysteriously disappear. I found a roommate to live with, even though I had never met her. Sally King was her name. I was told by a friend that she was a really nice girl who lived in an apartment in Ronks, Pennsylvania, and was looking for someone to share an apartment. I called her immediately, we chatted, and I made arrangements to move in with her.

On the following Thursday, just days after that miserable conversation with Mom, I dropped her off at the craft shop early in the morning. Then I did some fast work. Using a friend's pickup truck, I worked feverishly all morning, packing and loading everything I owned into that truck by myself. Bumping and dragging pieces of furniture down the short flight of deck stairs, I then propped, pushed and heaved them onto the back of the pickup. I felt so self-sufficient and strong, but now I realize that I was really very weak, and that my spirit was at a fragile point.

When I finally finished packing, I took one last glance around the apartment Mom had fixed for me. It was a beautiful living room, just recently painted and tastefully decorated to match the quaint little bedroom. This had been my haven, the place I loved and called my own. I also loved the small bathroom, where I had spent so many hours getting ready to go out with friends, agonizing over pimples and testing new makeup and beauty products.

Everything looked so empty now, as if someone had died. "Oh, well," I thought, "this part of my life has died. It's over, and that's that." I had convinced myself that Mom and Dad didn't want me or love me anymore.

Then came the hard part—I had to leave a note. What would I say and where would I leave it? Not on the kitchen counter, that would be too risky. The breeze blowing in through the screen door might whip it onto the floor, and they wouldn't find it. It was very important that my parents see the note, since I had resolved never to call them. I did not want to talk to them, or answer any questions, but I didn't want them to worry either.

I decided to leave the note lying on top of Mom's dresser, upstairs in their bedroom. I hurriedly wrote a jumbled message about living with a girl somewhere in the town of Ronks, that I couldn't take the fighting anymore, and they would be happier without me.

As I wrote, hot tears fell onto the paper. I quickly wiped them off, hoping they would not stain. Then I turned and stormed out the door.

"I wonder what it will be like living with Sally and finally being on my own?" I mused, as I turned right onto Route 23, leaving Churchtown behind. I floored the gas pedal, urging the work truck I was driving to get moving. I was eager to start my new life. Heading in the direction of Ronks, about a half-hour's drive, I settled into my seat, taking advantage of this time to think about my life.

My mind was swirling with thoughts of Mom...good old Mom. I tried to push those thoughts away. I really did not want to think about her. What would she feel as she read my note? I knew she'd probably cry, but that thought made me hurt inside and made me feel really sad. "It doesn't matter what she thinks," I argued, "It's high time she lets go of me. I won't be her baby forever."

I had such mixed feelings about my mother. She was a good mom to us kids, and ruled her domain with an iron fist and a crazy mixture of fun and humor. She had a fiery personality and a temper that was fearsome at times, but on the other hand, she was very enjoyable to be around. Time spent with Mom was never boring. She joined the family skating and sledding in the winter and went swimming and played ball with us in the summer, with lots of energy left over for baking, cleaning, cooking, mowing the lawn and helping in the barn. Mom excelled at everything she did on the farm. She tried to get as much out of every minute of every day as possible and wanted to experience life to its fullest.

I couldn't help but grin wryly as scenes from the farm days flashed through my troubled mind. "God must have a sense of humor," I thought, "Because the combination of my five brothers and my mom sure was a funny scenario to behold!" Her trusty yard-sticks were always handy and she broke more than a few on the backs of my fleeing brothers; but for the most part, the punishment was light compared to the thing that was done to deserve it. The stress those boys (and I) put our mother through was almost unbelievable.

I knew I would never forget the time Mom looked out her kitchen window on a Sunday afternoon to catch sight of several of her teenaged sons and a few of the neighbor boys running around the top of an open silo, sixty feet off the ground, as if it were a balancing beam on a playground. Her body was self-propelled out the door in two seconds flat and being helpless to do anything else, she opened her mouth wide and yelled at the top of her lungs, ordering her precious sons to get down off that silo immediately! They were safely on the ground in a few short minutes.

A very similar scene unfolded on another warm, summer day when Mom stepped outside the front door just in time to see my brother John and I precariously walking along the peak of the highest barn roof on the farm. It was times like these when her piercing voice could be heard echoing all through the small valley of Churchtown, and the neighbors were wondering what the Smucker kids were getting in trouble for. They would be sure to ask Mom later what the fuss was about, and to everyone's delight, she would relive the whole terrible episode to anyone who would listen, sputtering and fuming all throughout.

Of course, when there are a number of boys in one family, sooner or later one of them will get punished for something he didn't do. This was the case when Mom entered the basement to see fire burning in the wood stove (that no one except her or Dad was ever supposed to get near) and two of my brothers standing next to it. I watched wide-eyed and fascinated while she grabbed the closest boy and gave him a sound thrashing for playing with fire while the other son quickly escaped. After enduring his punishment, her unlucky victim was howling and saying, "It wasn't me; it was him!" Sighing, she shrugged her shoulders and apologized, knowing that she would never catch up to the guilty one, who could've been halfway out the field lane or down at the creek by then. Over the years we've all thoroughly enjoyed hearing her relate this story, throwing her head back and laughing while telling it.

I couldn't resist Mom's passion, humor and carefree spirit, and this was what pulled me in and made me love her even when things were bad between us. I had spent many days by her side and my mind was full of the memories we'd made together. Whether we were working, playing, laughing, arguing or just talking, time spent with Mom had always been stimulating and interesting. She had not been perfect, but had always been my friend, the light in my life. With an ache in my heart, I wondered how our relationship could have gotten so crazy over the last few years. How could two hearts be so intertwined and yet feel so far apart? How could we share so many similar passions and yet disagree on what I considered the "real" issues of life? We had been arguing and bickering so much lately that it was getting more and more difficult to remember the good times.

But it had not been that long before, just a few short years really, when Mom and I had been inseparable. I could always feel her delight in me: her little girl, her only daughter. She made my life exciting and adventurous with her boundless energy and charisma. Although I grew up with no sisters, I never felt that I had missed female companionship. Mom's love and attention satisfied me. In my younger years, I ran free on the farm with my brothers, but when I needed Mom, she was always there. Whenever she went shopping or visiting friends for the day, I got to tag along.

When I was a little older, she opened a three-story craft shop in the west end of our rambling farm house, in the old wash house. This interested me greatly, and I loved helping her with the crafts. I found myself spending more and more time by her side. We began going to numerous craft shows together, setting up huge displays of crafts to sell. The shows usually lasted two or three days. Sometimes we invited a friend, Miriam Reiff, the artist who did most of our paintings, to come along. Miriam would clear a space on one of the tables, and I watched in fascination as she painted. My heart swelled as I watched the colors swirl and flow together, forming beautiful works of art. I sat for hours breathlessly watching and learning.

On a warm summer day, at the age of thirteen, I was helping Mom with the cleaning, absently dusting everything in the kitchen. As I ran a damp cloth over an old, wooden box, my eyes rested on the cute little mouse face peeking out from behind a clump of strawberries that Miriam had recently painted on the box. I felt a sudden inspiration. Leaving my dusting cloth on the counter, I ran to find Mom. "May I borrow your paints?"

"Sure," she said, in a good-natured way. "Go right ahead."

I carefully carried her large box of paints and brushes out to the picnic table under the big Maple tree and got right to work. Eagerly, I created my very first painting, a perfect little mouse face, whiskers and all. My creation came effortlessly.

Ecstatic, I raced into the house, shouting for Mom to come and look at my artwork. Her face lit up as she admired the painting. Then she turned to me and said, "You are an artist! I'll put you right to work, and you will paint for me." She was as excited as I was, because the people who did painting for us were always falling behind and couldn't keep up with the orders.

So for the rest of the day, I tried my hand at painting several different subjects. Some of them were successful; others ended up in the trash. I fell into bed that night with a new excitement burning inside me and a new adventure on the horizon.

For many years, Mom and I were business partners. Whenever we did craft shows, she fixed a table for me with brushes, paint, and a small container of water. I painted items all day, drawing crowds of people to our stand and sometimes selling the products I painted before they dried.

I taught Mom to do decorative folk painting, and we spent days staining, painting, and varnishing all sorts of crafts to sell. There was a great demand for the items we were making, and we could hardly keep up. Mom did most of the housework, while I was kept busy filling the orders that came in. Sometimes I painted all day and late into the night. I became increasingly passionate about painting and disliked working at anything else.

Dad did not approve of my staying up late every night painting and then sleeping until nine o'clock in the morning. He thought I should have a "real" job, and insisted that I try something else for awhile. I finally yielded to his wishes. At the age of fifteen, I agreed to work at the Farmer's Market in Reading, Pennsylvania, selling cheeses, meats and barbecued chicken two days a week. I enjoyed the job, loved working with the public, and had many good times with my co-workers. Still, I found myself dreading the days when I would have to leave my beloved hobby of painting behind to go back to selling meat.

After a few months of working at the Farmer's Market, I quit and returned to full-time painting. I was back in the basement with Mom, doing what I loved and spending my time with her. We could talk about everything. I grew closer to her during our time of working together, sharing many of my dreams and ambitions.

But a few years later, Dad again insisted that I was getting "spoiled" with no schedule and no "governor," as he used to say. Upon his prompting I agreed to take a job at a sewing factory in Martindale. I strongly disliked sewing by piecework, and dreaded each day. I did not even last a few months there. After the job ended at the sewing factory, I took another job at Kitchen Kettle Village, working at the Funnel Cake House and Deli. Though not unpleasant, it left me feeling equally unfulfilled. Again, I longed to be at home painting.

One day, during my lunch break, I was casually walking around the small village, exploring all the familiar shops. Something bright caught my attention. At Parrot's Cove, a quaint, little tee-shirt shop, I saw someone painting pictures on shirts. I stopped and watched for a short while, thinking to myself, "I could do that." I dashed inside and asked if they needed a painter. Everyone looked at me in surprise. A clerk took in this excited, breathless, teenaged Amish girl and asked, "Can you really paint?"

Effortlessly, I painted a beautiful picture on a shirt for them. Before the end of the week I had the job. I was so happy, and so was Dad. Now he had me pinned down to a schedule, and I wasn't miserable. I stayed at the Parrot's Cove Tee-Shirt Shop for several years in my job as an artist and had a wonderful time with my co-workers and the customers.

I sat beside a big window to paint, drawing large crowds of silent admirers outside the window and into the store.

Brandishing a loaded brush, I thoroughly enjoyed hearing people gasp as I proceeded to splotch paint onto an unmarked white shirt. I also enjoyed answering the many questions about the Amish and chatted comfortably with everyone who came into the shop. Mom was so proud of my accomplishments, and I still spent some evenings and my days off by her side, painting crafts.

Mom and I enjoyed working together for many years, sharing so many likes and so many similar interests and traits. Thinking back on those years, I wondered where our relationship had gone wrong. How did our friendship get off track? I just could not imagine my life without her in it.

While I was reminiscing, my mind wandered to my new acquaintances. Surprisingly, I felt intimidated by them. Not many people made me feel uneasy or threatened, so why did these feelings keep coming to the surface? Some of the places I'd been to recently left me feeling unsettled. I knew that some of my new friends were snorting cocaine, and I had spied small bags of white powder a number of times. "Should I try some of these drugs?" I wondered.

I shuddered at the thought and tried to push the whole thing to the back of my mind. A part of me was curious, and wanted to experience the wonderful "high" that everyone was talking about. It did seem like a good way to escape the conflicting thoughts inside my head that were constantly warring for my attention. I had never been afraid to try new things before, so I repeatedly asked myself, "Why not try it just one time?" I had been toying with this idea for weeks, but the resistance I felt when it came to the idea of possibly getting hooked on drugs was stronger than my desire to do so. Just the thought of it left me feeling sick inside. "No," I firmly decided, "this is one door I will never open."

SECTION TWO

Rescued By Grace and Mercy

For You have delivered my soul from death, my eyes from tears, and my feet from falling.
(Psalms 116:8)

CHAPTER 6

On My Own

Spying Sally's house number, I looked around with interest. "Looks pleasant enough," I thought, as I pulled around to the back. "Oh, no," I groaned to myself when I saw the long flight of stairs leading up to the apartment on the second floor. I was reminded of all my earthly possessions that I had packed tightly into the back of the truck. Just the thought of dragging all that stuff up those steps made me weary.

Knowing that Sally was working and wouldn't be there when I arrived, I knocked on the door of her brother's house. John and his family lived on the main floor of the building, below the apartment. His wife Sarah came to the door and gave me the key to the apartment, so I could get some things unpacked before Sally came home.

Jogging up the stairs two at a time, I let myself in and curiously took in my surroundings. I was delighted. Sally had such an endearing way of decorating, and the small kitchen and living room seemed inviting and cozy. The sunlight wafting into the room made everything look bright and cheery.

Finding the empty bedroom that would be my new private space, I quickly took in the bland tan walls, uneven with several cracks running through them. I tried not to think about the beautiful, plum-colored walls in the apartment I'd left behind earlier today. "Was that just this morning? Seems like an eternity," I thought, glancing at the clock. "It is almost five o'clock. Mom will soon be getting home from the shop to read the note. Not something I want to think about now." So I pushed it out of my mind, focusing instead on the problem at hand.

How on earth was I going to get all my stuff into this tiny room? Thank goodness, my curtains and bedspread had some tan colors running through them so they would match the room. Being extremely color conscious, I knew I'd be miserable if things didn't match.

I had a few hours to sort through all my things and get settled before Sally came home, and was happy to be left alone as I worked. I had so many conflicting thoughts to sort through. This wasn't how I thought it would be. Feelings of anxiety rose up inside as I became increasingly unhappy with what I had done.

I normally enjoyed the excitement of small changes in my life, but as I continued unpacking the familiar items from home, my heart began to ache. This felt like a dramatic change to me, and I wasn't sure I was ready for it. As I found new resting places for each item and stuffed my clothing back into dresser drawers, I thought of home and my apartment there. Quickly, I pushed those thoughts away. "I'll learn to love it here," I whispered into the silence, "and pretty soon it'll feel just like home."

I heard a good-natured chuckle and looked up to see Sally, hand on her hip, leaning against the doorway. Her smile was pleasant, and I was immediately drawn to her. "Good, I think I'll like her," I thought with relief, admiring the pretty, pink dress she was wearing. "Wonder if she'll like me?"

"So you're Kathy?" she warmly greeted me, and we chatted for a good while, getting to know a little about each other. She struck me as being a friendly and open person. The twinkle in her eye and easy laughter were contagious, making me feel at ease. As we talked some more, I discovered that she attended the Spring Garden Church, the very church I had been wishing to visit.

Although I was still going to church with my family, I knew I wasn't right with God. It would only be a matter of time before another tidal wave of confrontations would bring on more confessions. Feeling powerless to reverse the direction of my life, I would have been happy not to attend any church; but Spring Garden Church was similar to ours in some ways, and seemed to offer the most possibility of finding what I was searching for. But my parents would not allow it, so the subject had been firmly closed.

I was excited to finally speak with someone who attended that church. I asked a flood of questions, gleaning any information I could about the congregation and the ministers. Sally invited me to go along with her on the following Sunday morning, and I eagerly accepted.

There was something so likeable about this girl. As we chatted easily and got to know each other better, I felt comfortable. It was as if I had known Sally for a long while. We were already becoming close friends. I wondered why she was so happy. The shine and sparkle in her eyes was enlightening and refreshing compared to the sadness that was so obvious in mine.

We chatted and rambled for a long while. I didn't even know this girl and she didn't know me. Somehow, she sensed that I needed to talk. Sally put aside any other plans she may have had for that day, and I had her full attention. Of course, she almost immediately asked why I decided to move away from my loved ones and home. I hesitantly spoke of the frustrations, anger and guilt I had been experiencing and the many conflicts I'd had with my parents. I also told her about the peer pressure I felt with my new friends and the confusion it all brought to my mind. She didn't hesitate to share her own personal story about a past filled with years of partying and all of the compromise that goes with that lifestyle. Sally shared with me how God's love had changed her and how abundant her life was now. She told me of her struggle with a heavy load of guilt. "What purpose did it serve?" she asked. "None. Guilt is a dead end street that leads nowhere. Guilt and shame lead to no real happiness, no real joy and no real purpose."

As she spoke, something was happening inside me. I realized in a moment that this was someone I could trust. I felt my spirit relax and let go of the tension that had constantly been present for weeks. I felt that Sally would understand me. All the feelings that I had shut up for so long came tumbling out in a rush of words and emotions. It felt good to release the negative thoughts and feelings I'd been holding onto so tightly. Talking to someone who understood me lifted the heaviness in my heart.

Sally and I talked many times over the next few days. I found myself being pulled in by her warmth, honesty and acceptance. The empty spot in my heart was being filled with good things. God was using Sally in her patient and gentle way to minister to my soul. Her lifestyle also appealed to me. There was an open honesty in everything she did—no secrets or lies, no hidden agendas and no games. Sally believed in truth and living a life that was full of joy. I wanted what she had. Once again, I felt that deep longing to be pure and free from sin.

The unrest I felt whenever I thought about my parents still tormented me. I missed them so much, but I convinced myself that they no longer loved me, that they were ashamed of me. I tried to get past needing their love and approval. I felt if I could just distance myself enough, the pain of missing them and needing them would eventually go away.

Sally's deep love and respect for her parents and family were obvious, and I could not help wondering if it had always been that way. With a heavy heart, I finally approached the subject with Sally that was the most difficult for me. Tears fell as I told her about how my parents hated me and no longer wanted me around, how they were ashamed of what I'd become. I told her how we couldn't agree on one thing.

Sally listened with a sober expression on her face, allowing me to empty myself. When I had no more words left to say, she leaned over close to me and looked into my teary eyes. Quietly, she said, "Kathy, I don't know your parents, but I know that they don't hate you." She continued, "Maybe they just care about you, and maybe they're worried about you."

She went on to tell me stories of how her older sister Maryann used to worry about her on the weekends, how she'd find her sister on her knees praying when she finally came home late at night. She told me of the occasional dreaded confrontations with her sister. She also shared how thankful she was that someone cared enough to worry about her, even if it meant that she would get upset or angry sometimes.

As I lay in bed that night, staring into the darkness, I had a whole host of new thoughts swirling in my mind. Silent tears rolled down my cheeks onto my pillow. I wondered if the things Sally had said were true. Could it be true that Mom and Dad actually cared about me that much? Could it be that worry and fear were driving my parents to react so harshly, even though they still really loved me?

If I were honest with myself, I knew my careless lifestyle was reason enough for worry. I also knew that the choices I'd been making lately were irrational and impulsive. And I had to admit to myself that many of those choices were made because I was trying to fit in with a crowd where I did not belong.

Then the tears began to flow freely, and the sobs that were caught in my throat broke free and escaped in long, shuddering gasps. The glob of emotions in the pit of my stomach churned and stormed relentlessly. The feelings of being misunderstood, angry, and confused were mingled with remorse and shame, and the weight of it all seemed to crush me.

In misery, I pulled the teal and burgundy comforter over my head, pressing the cotton fabric firmly over my mouth in an attempt to muffle the sound of my cries. I had thought I would be happy here, thought it would be better this way. Now I wasn't so sure. Each day as the sun went down, the darkness outside seemed to bring darkness to my heart. Something about the lonesome midnight hours in the unfamiliar bedroom made me feel so sad.

I also came to the full realization that the apron strings I was trying so hard to cut had not yet been severed. How could I be so angry with someone just a few days ago and miss her so much now?

CHAPTER 7

Remembering

The next day, I discovered I had failed to bring curtain rods. I contemplated going to a nearby store to buy new ones but then decided I could easily run home after work and retrieve the ones I had left there. Mom would be at her craft shop for the day, and what were the chances of Dad being at home? He rarely came home in the middle of the day.

Later that afternoon, after a day of painting tee-shirts at Parrot's Cove, I made the quick trip back home to get those troublesome old curtain rods. Pulling into the driveway I was relieved to see Dad's cattle truck wasn't there. "Good, the coast is clear," I thought. "Now I can just grab the rods and be on my way again."

I leaped up the back stairs in two easy strides and let myself into the kitchen. Ah, the familiar smells of home. "How can each home have its own special smell?" I wondered. It was a combination of Mom's flowers, with their sweet scent gently wafting in through the screen door, the dish soap we always used, and the faint smell of sewing machine oil. And, of course, there was the all-too-familiar smell of crafts and paint in the basement. "No time to stand and think," I chided myself. With a few short steps I reached my apartment door, right next to the laundry and front entrance.

The previous owners had made a small apartment on one end of the Cape Cod house where their elderly grandmother had lived. After we moved into the house, the apartment had become my private space, consisting of a bedroom, living room, bathroom and small kitchen.

Standing between the two doors, I remembered all the late nights, when hours past my curfew I tried to sneak in through those doors. I tried to be as quiet as possible so Dad would not hear me. It seemed no matter how quiet I managed to be, he always heard me and gave me lectures about the evils of late nights and the worries of having a teen-aged daughter out there alone. Usually I came back with a smart remark: "I'm not alone when I'm out there." Then he would give me another lecture about my choice of friends.

"Sorry, Dad," I whispered under my breath, as I pushed the door open into my apartment. I sucked my breath in as I took in the stark beauty of the room, so well arranged by Mom and me. Now it stood so empty. I wondered what Mom was going to do with my room. Maybe she would keep it empty, just in case I ever decided to come back home.

I pushed those thoughts out of my mind and was jerked back to reality. Why had I come here? Oh, yes, the curtain rods! There they were, right where I had left them. Grabbing them, I turned to leave but felt compelled to walk through my tiny apartment kitchen. Never having needed to use the kitchen for cooking or eating, this was where I had always come to satisfy my hunger for music. This was where I had spent hours communing with my Maker in the only way I knew how. Whether I sang the words of gratitude and praise or the sad and lonesome songs that I found in the church hymnal, the music lifted my spirits. Music always calmed the aching in my heart for a short while.

The small, brown table in the corner looked empty and bare without my collection of musical "toys" spread out on its surface. I had always cranked the music up with the use of a small speaker system. I used to hook a microphone to my brother's keyboard while singing my heart out. The music rang out through the entire house, but Mom and Dad didn't mind and always encouraged me to sing and play.

On the evenings when I was home, I spent many happy hours in this tiny kitchen, with the music, with the real presence of God that was there. Sometimes as I sang, I could feel a sense of my heavenly Father drawing me, urging me, and a deep longing would envelop me. In those times my heart swelled with many conflicting emotions. The thoughts I'd so successfully kept at bay would escape, running free in my mind, opening the floodgates to my soul. Without warning the tears would come so hard that I couldn't continue singing.

These were moments that no one else saw or knew about. People knew me as a joker, a fun-loving, rough-and-tough girl who would do anything. I usually threw caution to the wind and was happy and bubbly around other people. I felt happy in a rebellious, brazen sort of way, but still happy.

I tried to appear tough and hide my true feelings. I was also quick to demonstrate volatile and uncontrolled anger at the smallest problem. I was troubled by my lack of self-control, and the bouts of anger brought extreme feelings of self-hatred and hopelessness. I knew that I needed help, but I did not know where or how to find it.

Not knowing how to overcome the emotional responses and habits that were so ingrained, I suppressed and denied my feelings, refusing to deal with the dysfunctions in my life. I chose instead to block them out, pretending to care about nothing. On the surface, I considered myself completely fine and fulfilled. I thought I was enjoying the good things in life, so I wondered why these moments of raw pain and anger kept coming upon me. Why did I feel so sad and so vulnerable? And why did these uncontrollable moments happen while I was doing what I loved most?

While standing there alone in my apartment, the memories came in a flood. I always had such a deep love for music. As a little girl, I had memorized and sung many of the old hymns from beginning to end. I loved singing, and I sang wherever I went.

At the age of six, on the way home from a weekend getaway at a cabin in the mountains, our family stopped to eat at a restaurant. While we were waiting to be seated, I discovered an old piano in the corner of the antiqued room. I had never played a piano before, but I was curious about it. Fascinated, I easily plunked out the children's song, "Read Your Bible," as I softly sang the words. Then I continued playing the melody of every song I could think of until Mom came over: "It's time to eat with the rest of the family." As I walked away from that beautiful old piano, I took with me a new passion. That day I found a deep longing for a musical instrument, something I could use to play while I sang my favorite songs.

Every Christmas for the next several years was a bittersweet time for me. When Mom asked me what I wanted for Christmas, I always had the same request: "All I want is a keyboard."

Sighing, she wearily replied, "Kathy, you know our church doesn't allow musical instruments!"

I continued to beg and plead for a keyboard. Christmas day came each year, and I tried to hide my disappointment as I opened the beautifully wrapped packages, finding a doll-house one year and a typewriter the next year. I sadly plunked on the typewriter keys, wishing they would play music.

Finally, my mother grew tired of hearing me bellyache about a keyboard and gave me the liberty to buy an old portable organ at a flea market. For a few years, I enjoyed learning to play many new songs on the organ. Then, when my older brother Dave began attending a more liberal Mennonite church, Mom asked him if he would be willing to buy a keyboard. This would allow me access to a decent musical instrument, but officially our family would not own the keyboard. My brother agreed to purchase the organ, paying $100.00 for a keyboard he couldn't play so his little sister could fulfill a dream. My fingers caressed all those familiar keys as I joyfully played and sang all of the old hymns that I had memorized.

I loved that keyboard, but the way circumstances had evolved, I hadn't felt much like singing. For months before I left home, the house had been extremely quiet. The music in my soul had almost disappeared. That was a strange, new feeling for me. Several times I found Mom watching me with unspoken questions and sadness in her eyes. Then she would gently ask, "Kathy, why don't you sing anymore? I miss hearing you sing and play."

Musing over all these memories, I walked out of the apartment into the kitchen and through the screen door leading out to my car. My stomach growled, reminding me of how hungry I was. As I walked past the pantry, I couldn't help wondering if there were any crunchy or salty snacks in there. Better yet, maybe Mom had baked something. I yanked the doors open and was happy to find a big pack of chocolates. Yum! Mom and I were both serious chocolate lovers. I grabbed a handful of chocolates, and then spied some of her favorite snack crackers. "May as well take a pack of these, too," I decided, throwing everything into a little baggie. Turning to leave, I threw a few more pieces of chocolate into the baggie just for good measure.

Taking one last glance around the kitchen, I walked out the door and took a giant leap down the entire flight of stairs. "Good thing Dad didn't see that," I thought smugly. He always chided me for being such a tom-boy and pressured me constantly to start acting like a lady.

I rounded the corner, relieved to get out of there without any confrontations. Now I could quickly leave and no one would know I'd been there. I was happy to get away from all the familiar feelings and memories. "It's time to let go of my childhood and get on with real life," I thought as I approached my car. I suddenly felt eager to get back to my new home and hang the curtains in my room.

Just as I was ready to get into my car, I caught a glimpse of somebody walking around the side of the house. It couldn't be! Not... oh, no... but... it really was... Dad!

"Hello," he called out. I knew I couldn't just leave him standing there, so I turned to face him, keeping my eyes lowered. There was silence. I felt like a child who had gotten caught with her hand in the cookie jar. More silence. I could feel his eyes on me and wondered what his expression was. Was it anger, wrath or unforgiveness?

Reluctantly I raised my face and allowed my eyes to meet his. I dreaded seeing the disappointment I knew would be there, but even more than that, I dreaded having Dad see the guilt and confusion in mine. His eyes met mine for a brief moment, and then I watched as his gaze dropped down and rested on the sandwich baggie of crackers and chocolates that I clutched tightly in my hand. I felt so pathetic and miserable in that moment. Tears stung my eyes, threatening to erupt and spill over.

As my tear-filled eyes met his for the second time, I saw tears in his eyes too. I was surprised to see tenderness, mingled with love and sadness. Squinting into the sun and pulling his dark blue handkerchief from his pocket, he only said three sentences: "Kathryn, we want you to come home. We can work everything out. Just come home."

CHAPTER 8

Confrontation and Conviction

The weekend arrived, and Sally was gone for the evening. Saturday night had always been my favorite evening of the week. It was a night that promised excitement and fun times with close friends.

Somehow, I wasn't feeling excited or happy as I slipped out of my plain, homemade clothing and put on the outfit I had recently purchased at the Deb Store at East Towne Mall. Facing myself in the mirror, I took in my new image with one sweeping glance: a short, tight miniskirt, topped with a skimpy, red and white striped shirt. The outfit accented my shoulder-length brown hair.

I had always preferred shorter hair, not wanting to be bothered with a thick and cumbersome bun under my Amish head covering. When I took off the covering and the hairpins were taken out, a chopped, unruly, and slightly wavy mound of hair unraveled.

Lately, I had been exchanging my well-worn, homemade, Amish clothes for the newly bought outfits. I enjoyed shopping for new clothes and had a large collection of "worldly" attire that I was relying on more and more. My new wardrobe didn't cause me any guilt personally, but I was glad my father never saw me in those clothes. He didn't approve of the form-fitting way I made my homemade clothes and thought my dresses were too short at knee length. I paused in front of the mirror, thinking about the many times he had approached me on this subject. "So what would he think of me now?" I wryly asked myself, wincing at the thought as I glanced at the mirror again.

The doorbell rang, and I welcomed my friends with a smile. We agreed to order take-out food and enjoy a quiet evening at my new apartment to celebrate my newfound freedom.

I tried to settle in, but felt uptight and uncomfortable. Everyone else appeared to be relaxed. I munched on a cheese steak, loaded with sauce, peppers and onions. It was a great sandwich, especially when eaten with a big order of fries. We laughed and washed down our meal with ice-cold soda. I listened as my friends made small talk. Normally very talkative and outgoing, I didn't feel as if I had much to contribute to the conversation. I was aware of the six-packs of beer on the floor against the wall and knew the atmosphere would lighten up later on.

I ate until I was stuffed and was thoroughly engrossed in the movie we were watching. I was surprised to hear the doorbell ring again. "Who could that be?" I wondered aloud. I wasn't expecting anyone else to come by. Sighing, I pushed myself up and padded through the kitchen in bare feet, still wondering who could possibly be crashing our party. I pulled the door wide open, and the warm smile on my face quickly faded. I shrank back from the door, wishing I could disappear through a hole in the ground.

My first surprise came when I saw my father standing on the doorstep. Even more surprising was the sight of my older, married brother Dave. "Why on earth would Dave come along with Dad to see me?" I asked myself, not really able to come up with an answer. I rarely saw Dave and certainly never spoke with him about anything of importance.

My relationships with my beloved brothers had been almost nonexistent the last few years. All of them were disgusted with my constant arguments with our parents and surely they had heard many of the rumors about me that had been circulating in the church and in the community. Basically, my brothers ignored me. Long gone were the days when we'd been so close, and I stayed out of their way as much as possible.

But there stood Dave and Dad in the doorway. What did they want? Not knowing what else to do, I mumbled, "Hi! Ah... what d'ya want?" I felt embarrassed and awkward, wondering what they thought of my revealing choice of clothing. I hadn't felt self-conscious in this outfit before, but following their eyes suddenly made me wish I had a blanket to wrap myself in.

They made it short and sweet, barely staying ten minutes. I didn't invite them in and they didn't seem to mind. Both my father and brother urged me to come home, back to the shelter of family and love, back where I belonged. Then they turned and left as quickly as they had come.

I no longer heard the sounds of easy laughter and muffled voices coming from the next room. My jumbled thoughts were not making sense. All of the feelings and emotions that I had so carefully tucked away in the protection of defiance and denial were now pushing their way to the surface, breaking open the shell I had built around myself.

My hand still tightly clutched the doorknob, and I rested my forehead against the cold window pane. Warm breath escaped in quick, silent gasps, clouding the window. Staring into the darkness of the night, I watched the tail lights of Dad's car disappear out of the driveway.

Pieces of the short conversation we just had were playing over and over in my mind. I could hear the urgency in my dad's voice as he asked me to come back home. I could hear the honesty that was there when he said we could work everything out.

I wanted to believe that his words were true, but I remembered all the reasons I had left home and the recent and hurtful words my parents and I had exchanged. A voice inside was urging me to forget about them and all the heartaches that seemed to be associated with them, pushing me to go on with my plans of separation and independence. A part of me wanted to leave their control and authority far behind, but my heart was crying out for the protection and safety of home. I longed to be there again, and the homesickness I felt overwhelmed me. My immaturity was so apparent.

Everything within me wanted to dash into the night and run to my dad, to ask for his forgiveness and compassion once again. I longed to tell him how much I really did love him, how much I missed him, how much I missed being at home, even though it had only been three short days. I wanted to thank him for pursuing me, for letting me see the tears and tenderness in his eyes, and for being humble enough to beg his daughter to come back home. And I wanted to tell him that I, still a child, longed to do just that.

The rest of the weekend went by in a blur. Physically, I mingled with my friends, outwardly smiling. But mentally, I was far away, my thoughts troubled and unsure. I was sure of only one thing: I didn't belong where I was. I didn't want to be on my own anymore. Finally, I made the decision. I would go back home. Anxious anticipation almost immediately began to surge within me.

So just four days later, I moved back home. It was hard work, mentally and physically. It did not matter. I felt light and energetic. My apartment had never looked so inviting before. I could almost feel its warm embrace as I settled into the familiar comforts of home.

My newfound friendship with Sally had changed me, and it seemed as if our long conversations had "knocked some sense" into me. That is why I realize now that we can never underestimate the power of the simple words of a testimony.

The bond between Sally and me became strong and sure. On that warm summer day, when a lonely and confused teen-age girl was drawn into the life of a true friend and kindred spirit, something magical took place. From that point on, we were inseparable and spent every weekend together, becoming best friends.

I'm certain that Sally and I will remain friends for life, and will always reminisce about our providential meeting. We filled a void in each other's life, sharing many similar interests, including music. We sang together many times and became known for our harmonious voices that blended so well.

My parents were astounded and extremely happy to see the changes slowly taking place within their daughter's body, mind and spirit. They welcomed me back home with love and forgiveness. Although we still had plenty of disagreements and occasional battles of the will, the tension changed to an atmosphere of mutual respect. We found peace as a family, and Mom and I regained that special mother-daughter closeness.

I gained a new appreciation and respect for Dad too. His gentle, persistent love will always stay with me. Instead of see-ing him as a controlling father who didn't want his daughter to have any fun, I now saw the warmth in his eyes. His concern made me feel secure, for the first time in many long years. I realized that he provided a protective mantle over our home and family.

I love this story, and every time I tell it I am reminded that there is also a heavenly Father who is constantly watching out for His children. My parents, in great distress, thought their daughter had flung herself unprotected into a cold and dangerous world. But God, carefully watching, saw her plight and heard their prayers. In a tender movement of grace and love, He picked her up and carried her—to a tiny apartment in the town of Ronks, straight into the arms of an angel.

Thank you Sally, for being an angel of light and truth to me!

I was excited to attend the Spring Garden Church with Sally; it seemed to be just what I was looking for and just what I needed. I have been to a lot of churches, but this is one that will always hold a very special place in my heart. The people there were wonderful to me, and their kindness touched me in ways I hadn't been touched before. The love and acceptance they poured out to me was overwhelming. My spirit opened and blossomed into a beautiful flower during my time there. I can say that I really felt God's love, no longer just reading about it or merely talking about it, but could actually feel and understand it more fully because of the sympathetic compassion and approval those people freely gave.

I changed from the inside out. The restlessness and emptiness within were replaced with rewarding and fun relationships with Sally, Kate, Marian, Sill, and Leah. I thoroughly enjoyed the Youth Group, and my spirit was being filled with God's love!

The transformation didn't happen overnight, as it never does. But throughout the next year, although there were still many changes that needed to take place, I was loved with an unconditional love that saved me. Demonstrating the true love of Jesus, the people there met me right where I was, accepting me and all my problems. When I fell, they simply picked me up again and encouraged me to keep on going. Following their example, I learned how to reach out to God, openly and honestly communicating with Him. And I learned how to receive His grace and mercy.

Over time I developed my own convictions and found myself wanting to serve God, reverencing and obeying His commandments; and in so doing, discovered new pleasures in life that I'd never fully known before, in the form of holiness, purity and truth.

Eventually, the temptations that came no longer held me captive. As I submitted to God and His commandments, He covered me with His protection. I experienced a wonderful and liberating sense of freedom, after living under the bondage of guilt and condemnation for so long.

My prayer became similar to the psalmist's in Psalms 25:4-5:

> *Show me Your ways, O Lord. Teach me Your paths. Lead me in Your truth, and teach me, for You are the God of my salvation. On You I wait all day.*

And He answered me with the beautiful promise in Ezekiel 36:26-27:

> *"I will give you a new heart, and put a new spirit within you. I will take the heart of stone out of your flesh, and give you a [tender] heart of flesh. I will put My Spirit within you, and cause you to walk in My*

statutes, and you will keep My judgments and do them."

The few short years I was a part of the Spring Garden congregation helped me in building a firm foundation, preparing me for the months and years that followed. While there, my faith in God grew. My understanding of true Christianity deepened, allowing me to mature and grow in Him.

When Benji and I started dating he had already been attending a Mennonite church, and it was quickly decided by both of us that I would join him in attending there. I was saddened to say goodbye to the people who had become so familiar and precious to me, but it was never really a "Goodbye." Over the years I've continued in my previous friendships, and have always had a strong connection with the people there. Though crossing denominational lines, we'll always be a part of the same family...the family of God.

The freedom I found there is available to everyone. I know how depressing it is to never feel truly "good" about oneself. I also know what it feels like to enjoy the momentary pleasures of sin, only to be left carrying a heavy load of guilt for years afterward. This is how the devil robbed me of the full blessings of God for a long time. God cannot and will not fully bless a life that is trashed and littered with hidden sin. Proverbs 3:33 warns us that *"The curse of the Lord is on the house of the wicked."* I falsely believed that I could gratify my deepest desires with the empty pleasures of this world.

But there is no pleasure and no joy that transcends the pleasure of feeling the blessings of God on my life. He is a vital part of every human being's needs, and I could never be fully satisfied without Him. Only God can save us from enduring unfulfilled and unfruitful lives. Only He can grant us eternity with Him, and without Him we are so lost. Yet *"The Lord is near to all who call upon Him, to all who call upon Him in truth. He will fulfill the desire of those who fear Him; He also will hear their cry, and save them."* (Psalms 145:18-19)

One lesson I have learned well is this: that the people I associated with heavily influenced my decisions, either weakening or strengthening me. 1Thessalonians 5: 22 warns us to *"Abstain from every form of evil."* As long as I insisted on associating with ungodly people, there were constant temptations. The first logical thing to do was to cut off those unhealthy relationships. When I surrounded myself with godly people and friends, it was so much easier to say "No!" to the temptations that came. Their influence strengthened me, and I gained the confidence to change my direction, and reach out for something so much better.

Although my new friends and the people at church made a significant difference, it still came down to God and me alone. Ultimately, I wasn't able to depend on anyone else to make the right choices for me or to hold my hand twenty-four hours a day, seven days a week. I needed to find my own, true identity in Christ. And that is why the promises and life-giving words in the Bible became so valuable to me, giving me the ammunition I needed to break the devil's hold on me, rendering satanic forces powerless.

I finally felt connected to God, could feel His power, and could say with confidence that my life was taking a different direction.

SECTION THREE

Forgiven, Redeemed and Loved

Bless the Lord, O my soul, and forget not all His benefits; who forgives all your iniquities, who heals all your diseases; who redeems your life from destruction; who crowns you with loving kindness and tender mercies; who satisfies your mouth with good things…. (Psalms 103:2-5a)

CHAPTER 9

Finding Love

At the age of twenty-two, I married the man who truly is my soul mate and best friend. It was seventeen years ago, at the time of this writing, that we began our journey together. Those years have been fun, exciting and rewarding. From the early stages of our friendship, we enjoyed a close bond, which later blossomed into intense and passionate love for each other. Benji is several years older than me, and has been a friend of my older brothers since I was fourteen. I didn't pay much attention to my brothers' friends and can't remember getting to know Benji until I was fifteen years old.

My parents owned a small, rustic cabin at the foot of a small mountain in a secluded wooded area in Elverson. It was a great place to hold gatherings, and my parents occasionally invited the church youth group and several families from church to the cabin for an afternoon and evening of food, volleyball and the exciting game of pitching quakes.

On one such occasion, a beautiful Sunday afternoon, I was helping Mom prepare a large meal inside the cabin as the youth began arriving. I was excited to see some of my close friends had been invited, and we chattered happily as they joined us in the kitchen, setting out steaming bowls of hot food for the mid-day meal.

After everyone had eaten their fill, we washed and dried the stacks of dirty dishes in the tiny kitchen. With nothing better to do, we then took a short walk into the woods surrounding the cabin, talking and laughing about the day's happenings.

Spying my brothers, John and Andy and their friends on the path ahead of us, we yelled, "Hey, wait up!" and ran to catch up with them. I didn't know the other guys too well, but I had seen them with my brothers at church, and they'd been to our house numerous times. Knowing little about the boys except their names, we had a few awkward moments and lulls in the conversation.

"We're going for a long hike into the woods, and you girls can tag along if you aren't sissies," the boys said, chuckling and grinning at each other. That was all we needed to hear. My friends and I, feeling we were anything but sissies, followed hot on the boys' heels.

We walked for several hours and were gone for most of the afternoon. Deep in the forest, we encountered numerous obstacles. There were streams to cross, fences to climb and gullies to jump. Having grown up in the shadows of five robust, rowdy boys, I heartily welcomed each new challenge, rudely turning down any attempts my brothers made to help me.

Several times I fell behind and noticed that one of the guys, Benji, always waited for me. We chatted easily as we caught up with the rest of the group. At times he offered his hand to give me a lift up steep hills or through rough terrain. Although I was known as a self-sufficient tomboy who refused help from anyone, I suddenly became very needy and readily accepted Benji's hand every time he extended it to me.

I became more and more aware of him and less aware of anyone else in the group. I felt an instant attraction to Benji. I felt a compatibility that was too strong for coincidence. I could not deny the strange whirl of feelings within and was startled by their intensity.

Hours later, after the group had hiked almost all the way back to the cabin, we stopped to take a break, resting against trees, stumps and logs. Everyone chatted aimlessly, feeling great about our long and adventurous hike. Then I observed the strangest thing. Stretched across a creek nearby, about three feet above the water was a thin steel pipe, five or six feet across. It looked as if it had been put there as an aid in crossing the creek, but anyone could see that it would be impossible to balance on that narrow, slippery pipe.

Upon closer inspection, I noticed a wire fence running beside the pipe and quickly decided it would be fun and challenging to attempt walking the pipe while holding on to the fence. Never mind the Sunday dress I had on or the fact that I was a young lady budding into womanhood. Strolling over to the pipe, I announced boldly, “I’m going over. Who’s coming with me?” A few people gasped, and others started telling me how crazy this idea was. This only made my desire for the adventure stronger. As I stepped gingerly onto the pipe, I heard a loud voice say, “I’ll go with her.”

Quickly, I spun my head around, not daring to believe it was Benji, but, yes, it was. My heart skipped a beat as he stepped forward. I searched his face to see if he was joking. I wasn’t disappointed, because the look in Benji’s eyes said it all. I knew I had some competition here.

The rest of the group looked on breathlessly, sure that we would both end up falling into the water below. But with determination and lots of laughter, slipping, sliding, and clutching fiercely to that wire fence, we managed to get safely across and back again.

Years later, Benji and I still talk about that incident and can remember how we laughed so hard our sides hurt during that slow trek across the pipe. To make matters worse, every time Benji thought he was going to fall, he would reach out and grab onto me, because he was not about to go down alone and admit defeat to a girl.

Our daredevil stunt was outrageous and hilarious. The thought of Benji competing with me and ruthlessly picking on me, even though I was a girl, struck me as extremely humorous. As usual, when challenged, I fought back like a tiger, struggling to keep him far behind me. Being in such precarious positions, we both nearly collapsed several times from laughter.

The remainder of the day passed in a haze. The creek crossing with Benji had been a great adventure, and I was in love. "Hmm..." I thought, watching him, "Daring, fun, adventurous, competitive, not afraid to try new things, and yet so sweet, not to mention good looking and athletic. This person seemed almost too good to be true."

I was disappointed when the day was over and never looked at Benji the same again. I fell into bed that night with a sigh of contentment. I had sweet dreams about his teasing grin, the soft expression in his light brown eyes, and the loud, raucous laughter we had shared while crossing that slippery old pipe.

I breathed a prayer into the darkness that night and countless nights after, a prayer that I will always remember and cherish. With all my heart, I prayed, "Lord, let me marry Benji someday."

Since he was close friends with my brothers, Benji became a frequent visitor at our house. Although we both went on to pursue other relationships, we were constantly reminded of the fact that our feelings for each other were strong. Both of us knew we were too close, talking too much, and spending too much time together to be "just friends."

Benji was always the one person who could make me laugh and make me feel happy, and being with him made me feel complete. The problems I was facing and the inner struggles would fade away into the distance when he was near me. Our hearts were beating to the same rhythm, and our spirits were connecting more each time we were together. Without realizing it at the time, Benji and I were falling deeply and hopelessly in love with each other.

We were not free to talk about our feelings, so we found other ways to express our love. Even though we did not say the words, our eyes constantly met. Our gazes locked. The messages we sent to each other were strong and sure.

We shared a restlessness, a stirring within and melancholy feelings of never being quite satisfied. When we were together, those feelings were replaced with deep contentment and peace. I came to realize there was no one in the world I would rather be with than Benji. I knew he felt the same way about me.

But things were getting more and more complicated in my personal life. Trying to find a way to escape the restlessness and discontent in my heart, I opened many doors of temptation. Instead of relying on God's love and guidance to lead me, I chose to become self-reliant instead. I allowed rebellion to drive me, influencing my thoughts and actions.

Looking back at this time in my life, I realize that my arrogance and sin were the very things that kept Benji and me apart for so long. He was watching me closely, watching me break off one relationship after another, watching me act irrationally and impulsively, watching my tender heart grow cold again. My actions built a huge wall of mistrust between us.

Although Benji never stopped loving me for a minute during this crazy, rebellious time in my life, the warmth and camaraderie we once shared was now tainted. How could he trust me? I became disheartened as I felt more and more empty inside. My heart ached with longing and love for him, but I didn't belong to him. I shouldn't have been thinking about him, but I could not seem to find happiness with anyone else.

After I was excommunicated from the church for the second time, I was out of options or plans, having no idea what I would do next. I felt that I was living under the cloud of other people's expectations, judgments and punishments. Because of my past failures, I fully surrendered to feelings of inadequacy and inferiority. I did not know what the future held for me. I could not go back to being who I was before, but the future was blocked with uncertainty. It was as if I was frozen in time.

I hadn't seen or spoken with Benji in quite a while and was happy to bump into him in town one Saturday night. Grinning, he leaned over to open the passenger door of his car and yelled, "Get in. It's great to see you." I was happy to oblige and sank gratefully into the warmth of his sports car, a sleek, black Monte SS. The smell of Benji's favorite cologne and his friendly grin aroused familiar, bittersweet feelings. I slouched a little lower into the seat, my gaze resting on the stereo lights. We sat in silence for a few seconds, listening to soft music wafting gently into the air.

I smiled to myself, knowing that Benji didn't like blaring music, preferring to keep it in the background. I liked loud music, and he and I had often had power struggles over the volume of music in his car. I loved to crank it up, only to have Benji quickly reach over and turn it down. This usually went on until I gave in. After a few spiteful words from my corner, we would both end up in comfortable laughter.

I felt his eyes on me and longed to meet his gaze, but could not bring myself to look him in the eye. I normally felt at ease with Benji, and we could always talk about anything. But now I felt ashamed and unworthy, wishing I had not disappointed him. I knew Benji was far from perfect, but also knew he wouldn't do the things I'd been doing.

Staring at the blinking stereo lights, I hesitantly spoke into the darkness. "So why did you open the car door for me? Why'd you even let me in? You know I'm excommunicated from church for good, now." Sarcastically, I added, "I'm a disgrace, ya know." Sighing, I said the words I didn't want to admit, "Guess I've messed up my life, huh?"

There was silence, but I knew Benji was just contemplating everything I had said. He often did that when we had serious discussions. He was a deep thinker and did not answer hastily, weighing his words first. I liked that trait in him; it made me feel that he cared about what I had to say.

But I wasn't so sure I wanted him to think too deeply about my messing up my life. "Oh, well," I thought gloomily, "What does it matter what he thinks anyway?" I tried to convince myself I didn't care and felt the cold winds beginning to blow across my heart again. Consciously numbing the pain I knew would come with his answer, my eyes rested on the door handle. I wondered if I should just open the car door and leave before Benji could answer or stay and endure the criticism.

I'd gotten good at walking away from situations that were difficult or uncomfortable. Now, my first instinct was to run from Benji as well. I was tempted to listen to the voices inside my head, urging me to leave before he could answer my question; the voices that were reminding me that most likely Benji didn't really care about me anyway.

My thoughts conflicted wildly in my mind; but this felt different from the other times I'd walked away from people. Something was holding me there, and I knew I needed to stay to hear Benji's reply, whether it was positive or not. Although several of our heated discussions had not ended well during the last year, somehow I knew I could trust him to tell me the truth. I also knew that I was desperate to hear the words he had to say.

Squirming uncomfortably in the leather bucket seat, I kept my focus on the door handle. As Benji spoke, I could not believe what I heard. His words penetrated my aching heart, soul and spirit. Calmly and softly, he said, "Kathy, it doesn't matter who you are today. I see the person that you want to be and the amazing person you're going to become."

There was only the sound of soft music playing as his words hung in the air. Silently, I processed Benji's response. Had I heard him correctly? Did he actually feel that way about me? Could he possibly know how much I wanted to be a good person? How did he know that I desperately needed to hear those words?

Now my eyes eagerly found his, and we openly searched each other's faces, our eyes locking and holding each other's gaze. Hungrily I drank in the tenderness, the grace, and the love that was there. My heart sang as I realized the depth of Benji's feelings for me.

Like a cork being released from a bottle, my feelings and thoughts came out in a rush. We talked and talked. He encouraged me in every way and gently reminded me of the good things in life, urging me to make a change for the better.

I came away that night with a spring in my step and fire in my heart! And I'll never forget the impact those words had on my life: "It's not who you are today; it's the amazing person you're going to become."

CHAPTER 10

First Dates and Romance

It wasn't until I was nineteen and Benji was twenty-one that we officially started dating. I needed to begin making right choices, and he needed to know that he could trust me before we could have a true relationship. It hurts me still to know that it was my wrong choices and actions and the sin in my life that kept Benji from seriously pursuing me all those years. Not knowing how much he loved me, I believed the opposite. The pain of believing that we didn't share the same feelings caused me to act out in ways I wouldn't have otherwise.

Emotionally, we played cat and mouse, confusing each other beyond words, all the while claiming to be "just good friends." Misunderstandings can absolutely destroy God's plans, and that is why open and honest communication is so valuable and important.

Benji finally talked to the wrong person, or should I say the right person, about his feelings for me, being completely honest with someone for a change. Unknown to him the girl he confided in was a fairly close friend of mine. I had spoken to her several times about my feelings for Benji. Sensing the heartache we were both carrying and not knowing what else to do, she let me know that Benji and I needed to talk. We still laughingly thank her today for getting us together.

Benji and I met to talk at Two Cousins Pizza on a pleasant summer evening. I still remember sitting across the table from him in the corner booth of that little restaurant, taking in his smooth, tanned face and broad shoulders. He and I were ready to be honest and open with each other.

We discussed many things: all the misunderstandings we'd had, all the questions that we wanted to ask, and the feelings we still had for each other. It felt good to be honest, to come out and say things I had wanted to say for years. I felt complete and satisfied when I was with Benji. I was not very accustomed to these feelings, and relished every minute we had together.

We were still there in the parking lot an hour after the pizza place had closed for the night. Benji watched with amusement on his face as I tried to balance on a thin slab of concrete that was there. He made smart comments, telling me, "If you don't watch out, you'll fall and break your neck!" I laughed loudly, reminding him sarcastically of my great agility and sure sense of balance. Just like always, we were goofing around and competing against each other. This was part of the fun in being together for us, and the humor ran high.

He reminded me of the time he heard me bragging at a youth function about how I could run like a deer. I had continued my stream of ranting, informing my friends that after sixth grade I had beat everyone in the school races. This got Benji's hackles up, and he said, "You won't ever beat me."

I laughed him to scorn. "You're completely ridiculous if you think for one minute that you can run faster than I can."

"You're totally out of your tree if you think you could ever outrun me," he countered.

So this led to a big race, with the entire youth group cheering us on. I was quite confident, never doubting myself for one second. But Benji won and not just by a little. He was way ahead of me when he flew through the finish line. I couldn't believe it. Oh, that burned me up, but I had to admit defeat.

He can still run faster than I can, and it still makes me bristle. I guess I should have known better than to challenge him, since he was involved in every possible sport at school. As a teenager, he excelled in all sports. If the truth be told, I was actually proud of him and greatly admired his swiftness and determination. His schedule was always packed with hockey games, racquetball practice, volleyball tournaments, soccer matches and baseball games.

Shortly after the evening we enjoyed together at Two Cousins Pizza, Benji went on a mission trip for three months to the Peten Jungle in Guatemala. It was a long three months, but I knew he was coming back to me. I wondered what it would be like dating Benji. I could not imagine how wonderful it would be to go places together and hear him say the words, "I love you." I wondered what it would feel like saying those words to him. I thought about Benji constantly while he was gone.

Soon after the three months were over and Benji came back safely to Pennsylvania, there were revival meetings at West Haven Church, the church we had both previously attended. Mom and Dad asked me to come with them. Although I was no longer attending this church, I decided it would be fun and interesting to go back there for a visit. Benji knew I was going and decided to come too. It felt good to go back, and we both enjoyed the service.

Afterward, I noticed Benji having a conversation with my father in the church lobby. Dad had a huge grin on his face. I knew how much he liked Benji and enjoyed talking with him, so I didn't give it much thought. In the parking lot, Benji and I spent some time together, just talking. I was disappointed when he left, saying he needed to get to bed early.

Later, I found out why Dad looked so happy in the church lobby talking to Benji. Benji was asking my dad for permission to date his daughter. Of course, my father joyfully said, "Yes." We had our first date a short while later.

Our first official date was at the Olive Garden® for dinner. What an amazing evening. Our opposite characteristics emerged on the first date. To me, this was a fancy restaurant, as opposed to a hamburger joint. I usually found formal restaurants stifling, preferring light and casual atmospheres where no formalities are required. I quickly discovered that Benji is just the opposite. He enjoys peaceful, quiet dinners at elegant places. I found out that although he does not desire to live daily life in a prim and proper fashion, Benji has a deep appreciation for the finer side of life.

Benji's gentle spirit brought peace to my mind, and I realized that I could always find an inner sense of calmness when we were together. While Benji has always had a calming effect on me, I've brought a craziness and excitement into his life.

I'm still not sure that he always welcomes my extreme behavior, but he did chuckle on the way home that evening, when in the warm seclusion of his car, I flung aside my high heels. Feet on the dashboard and head resting lazily on the back of the leather bucket seat, I sighed loudly, enjoying the casual and relaxing drive home almost as much as I had enjoyed the quiet dinner.

We dated for a year and a half, and our love grew stronger every day. From the first date, it always seemed as if I was dating my best friend. In reality I was. Of course, my other friendships were still important to me. My girlfriends and I still hung out and did lots of things together.

Benji didn't feel the need to call or see me every day, and I liked it that way. He gave me the space I needed. Our time together was quality time. I was happier than ever before in my life and felt deeply satisfied. I finally had peace, perfect peace.

Maybe it's because we're both the youngest in our families, but it seemed Benji and I were never together very long before we were pushing, challenging each other and constantly teasing. Take, for instance, one evening when I was out shopping, and Benji was running errands. We happened to meet at the Getty in town on the way home. It was a pleasant surprise, to be sure. We leaned against our cars, talking.

Soon we tired of standing but weren't yet finished with our endless rambling. Lying on our backs on a strip of grass beside the Getty, we gazed through the glare of the street light above to the stars in the sky, talking and laughing for hours into the night. As always, we eventually got into a tiff, some crazy debate. Quickly standing up, I towered over him. Grinning down on him, I said smartly, "I should just walk away from you and let you sit here all by yourself. That'll teach you not to argue with me."

He quickly retorted, "You can't get away. I'll just come with you."

I stupidly answered, "You couldn't catch me!" Wrong thing to say...the chase was on. I got a head start, taking off like a bat. I ran screaming and shrieking at the top of my lungs across the street, then over to the motel behind an old country-style restaurant, with Benji hot on my heels. Oh, the sheer terror of being chased was so exhilarating, and my heart felt as if it would pound out of my chest. Coming to the outside stairway leading up to the second floor, I clambered up those steps as fast as I could, stifling the screams so I would not wake peacefully sleeping tourists just inside the motel.

On the fourth or fifth step Benji's hand gripped my left ankle. Like a vice grip, he held me hostage. My heart raced as I realized I was caught. Collapsing onto the steps, I surrendered completely as his arms lovingly surrounded me. Loudly gasping for air, we laughed and laughed, sitting together on those rickety old steps in the wee hours of the morning.

As always, Benji had won, and I had to admit defeat. But in the safety and strength of his arms, I didn't mind at all. This is where I wanted to be. This is where I felt safe. As he held me closely, passionately, I could feel his heart beating with mine, and I loved him so much in that moment.

CHAPTER 11

Wedding Bells!

I was ready to get married. I would have said, "Yes" to Benji's proposal after the first date, had he asked me. I was getting impatient after dating for a year and a half. Benji had already bought a house and was living in it at the wooded property he owned in Narvon, Pennsylvania. We spent a lot of time there, clearing out trees and cleaning up the large, rambling thirteen-acre property. I grew to love it there and dreamed about living there someday.

But it seemed to me as if we were bound to date forever. And my pride would have never allowed me to bring up the subject. It was far beneath me to ever let Benji know that I was desperate to finally be his wife. Secretly, I was hoping and praying that Benji would propose soon.

We did a lot of activities together, but we never needed much to satisfy us. Our favorite date was, and still is, going to a nice restaurant to eat and talk. We usually spent the remainder of the evening at his house, relaxing in a quiet and peaceful atmosphere.

On such an evening, a cool April night, we had eaten and were happy to be back in the comfort of the small, cozy house in the woods. I was tired. Sighing loudly, I sank into the soft couch. Yawning lazily, I stretched my arms high above me and watched Benji as he lit a fire in the fireplace, making the atmosphere warm and glowing.

My mind wandered, and I tried to shut out the thoughts that were coming more and more these days. How nice it would be to stay here, never to leave again, but to call this home! I could hardly imagine the joy of sharing every minute of our lives together, sharing a home, and waking up to his teasing grin every morning. We never wanted to leave each other after the evenings we spent together and always clung to each other as long as we could. Benji dreaded dropping me off at home, then going back to his house alone, and was becoming more verbal about his feelings as time went on. "So what are we waiting for?" I silently wondered.

As the fire crackled to life, I watched him sweep up the small pieces of wood and ashes on the floor, admiring how he always did everything with excellence and neatness—the exact opposite of the way I did things. I shuddered as I thought about the way my room looked much of the time. Too busy and excited about doing creative things, I had a strong dislike for housework. I had a bad habit of throwing everything onto a heap, not cleaning up after myself, and leaving a train wreck of a mess wherever I went. I knew I needed to discipline myself in this area, especially with marriage so heavy on my mind. "But who knows how long it'll go on before he ever gets around to asking me," I thought gloomily.

Pushing those thoughts aside, I focused on the present moment instead. Glancing at the clock, I was disappointed to see it was already getting late. I felt the familiar feelings of discontent again, the restlessness coming over me in waves. My mind was already made up. There was no one else for me but Benji. And I knew that he felt that way about me too. So to me, it was as simple as that. If we both knew that we loved each other, what could possibly be standing in the way?

As Benji wandered over to the kitchen to snap off the lights above the sink, I leaned back into the couch and closed my eyes. Hearing him coming back into the living room I kept my eyes closed, anticipating his presence beside me and the warmth of his arms that I knew would surround me.

But when he didn't move in beside me, I opened my eyes. I was surprised to see him kneeling on the floor in front of me. Our eyes met, and in a flash I knew that this was the moment. My breath got stuck in my throat, and my heart did flip-flops. I heard him slowly and softly speak the words, "Kathy, I love you more than anyone in the world. I want you to be my wife. Will you marry me?"

Although there was no music playing, I could hear it in my spirit, a wondrous and beautiful chorus swelling and flowing with the wild beating of my heart. The hunger, the desires and the deep longings within were finally being satisfied with a love that would prove to exceed my wildest dreams.

I believe the angels were rejoicing that night as God's ultimate plan for us was beginning to unfold. We were not able to see how much we would need and complete each other in the days and years to come, nor could we see the strength and wholeness we would both receive from the other. And there was no possible way for me to know that night how Benji's gentleness, patience and insight would be a powerful aid in bringing healing to my wounded and broken spirit in the following years. I could not know that God had given him to me to be my rock, to give me love as I never knew before, and to walk close beside me as I found true victory in my life.

All I knew in that moment was that a prayer I breathed into the night six years earlier, at the tender age of fifteen, was finally being answered. Benji, still on his knees offered me his hand, and I clasped it tightly in mine. I cried tears of joy. I couldn't stop crying as he scooped me up into his arms and smiled tenderly at me. In a moment of true and pure commitment to each other, we freely and openly gave our hearts to each other, our spirits connecting on a deeper level than ever before.

When Benji made a decision, he moved ahead very quickly. Our wedding was no exception. He wanted to be married in three short months. I didn't care when or where we got married. It could have been the next day in a barnyard, as far as I was concerned. We agreed that a three-month engagement was proper and then happily began making wedding plans.

We were married on July 9, 1994, the hottest day of the year, at Victory Chapel in Paradise, Pennsylvania. It was beautiful outside, and the day flew by in a haze. The wedding ceremony was a wonderful experience. Walking down the center aisle arm-in-arm with my father, my heart was beating wildly. My breath came in short, happy gasps. I couldn't believe this day had finally come, and I was fully embracing every minute of it.

Dad passed me over to Benji and turned to sit down, but I didn't realize the significance of that moment until later. My father must have had mixed emotions, giving the hand of his daughter to another man, knowing Benji would be taking on the responsibilities he'd carried for so many years. But after all the heartache I'd put him through, he must have felt some relief, too!

We had a short memorial service for Benji's brother, Elmer, who had passed away years earlier. It was touching and sad. Benji wiped tears from his eyes, because he had always thought he would have his beloved, older brother Elmer standing beside him as best man.

Sadness turned to joy as family and friends celebrated our love. Standing next to Benji's tall form, in the midst of people who loved both of us, my heart leapt with joy and happiness. As we spoke our wedding vows and gazed into each other's eyes, I could see a beautiful and happy future together. I just could not wait to begin life as Mrs. Benji Smoker.

At the reception we enjoyed the delicious meal Mom had prepared. Then my new father-in-law, Ben Smoker, prayed a special prayer to bless our marriage. The prayer was a perfect close to the day. As I watched my father-in-law bow his head in prayer, I remembered the warm, summer evening when I'd nervously faced him from across the old picnic table, and he had offered such powerful counsel without judgment or condemnation. I thanked God for the overwhelming love and grace I had experienced that evening. Then I thanked Him for the wonderful changes that had taken place in my life, for bringing me into this special family, and for bringing me to this joyous day.

After bidding our families goodbye, I was relieved to escape into the quietness of the limousine awaiting us in the parking lot. It felt so good to be finished with all the formalities. Finally, I could stop smiling that frozen smile for the cameras and kick off my high heels. I sank into the soft seats of the limousine. At last, I was alone with my new husband.

I will never forget how God began working powerfully in my life, giving me the deepest desires of my heart—including a wonderful, loving and caring husband—when I started making the right choices and walking closer to Him. I paid a high price for my carelessness, and there were several lost years of my life that were unfruitful because of making wrong decisions. Unfortunately, this time 'down the drain' could have been so full of power and promise.

I know that many people can identify with me in this area, and feel as if they have lost a portion of their lives to the destruction of sin or deep hurts. That's why it is important to claim the promise God gave us in Psalms 23:3: *"He restores my soul; He leads me in the paths of righteousness for His name's sake."* I found that it is never too late to make a fresh start and fully surrender the past, present and future to Him. The Word says we can take comfort in knowing that He is a God of restoration and new beginnings. God promises in Joel 2:25: *"I will restore to you the years that the swarming locust has eaten."* What was intended for evil can always be used to produce positive results by the power of Jesus who lives within us: *"And we know that all things work together for good to those who love God, to those who are called according to His purpose"* (Romans 8:28).

There are so many verses in the Bible that remind me of my full value and worth through the redemption of Jesus Christ. It doesn't matter that I most definitely have not always lived in His perfect will. When the ghosts of the past come to haunt me, I can say assuredly, *"If anyone is in Christ, he is a new creation; old things have passed away; behold, all things have become new"* (2 Corinthians 5:17). Philippians 1:6 also reminds me that the work God started in me will come to full completion: *"Being confident of this very thing, that He who has begun a good work in you will complete it until the day of Jesus Christ."*

The enemy may come like a flood and try to persuade us of our uselessness due to an imperfect and marred past, but we can silence those negative voices with these verses. When God's Word is in our hearts, His Spirit rests upon our souls and guards the doorway to our thoughts with truth and might. *"When the enemy comes in like a flood, the Spirit of the Lord will lift up a standard against him"* (Isaiah 59:19b).

With these promises in my memory, I am always mindful of the fact that my value and worth is not based on past mistakes. Rather, my true identity is found through Jesus' love for me and His blood that was shed for my redemption. When He rose from the grave and broke the chains of death, all of mankind received the free gift of His power. This power enables me to overcome the sins of the past and gives me strength to walk in newness of life.

> *"Just as Christ was raised from the dead by the glory of the Father, even so we also should walk in newness of life"* (Romans 6:4b).

Picture
Album

Left to right: Lester, Dave, Sam holding me, Andy, John

My baby picture, 1972

The farmhouse we grew up in

9 months old

Brothers John and Andrew: cousin Rueben Esh and me sitting in the wheelbarrel

John, me and Andrew

Holding my puppy

Playing with the kittens in the barn

Landis Hill School, where I attended grades 6-8

Mom, John, Dad, Andrew, me and Lester

The teen years

Playing keyboard
after the car accident

My dear friend Sally

One of my paintings

Painting tee-shirts at The Parrots Cove

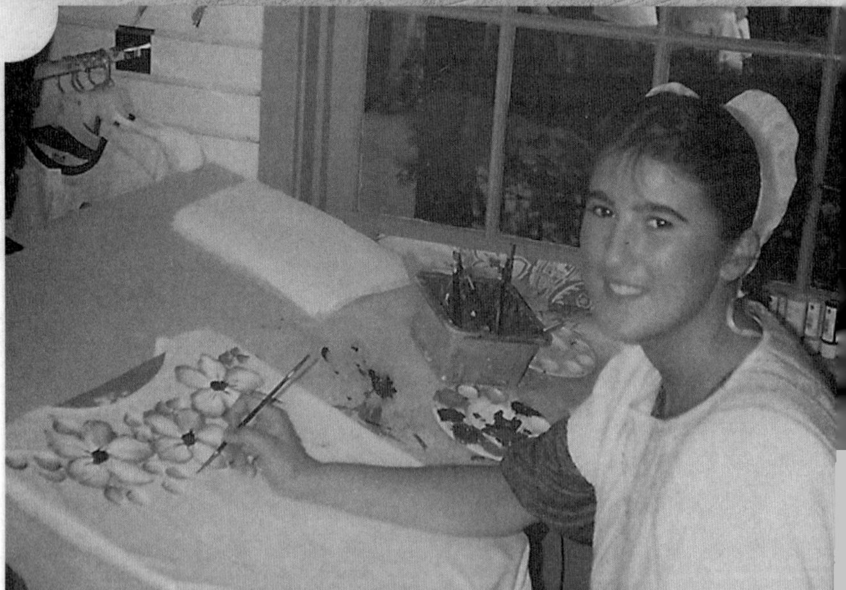

Benji and me – dating days

Wedding Day – 22 years old

Newlyweds

Breakthrough's Gospel Crusade in Africa

I loved the children in Africa

Sherry and me teaching Sunday school

The Breakthrough band – 1997

The Breakthrough band – 2011

Family photo – Ana, Janelle, Benji, Kathy, Sari, Jessica

SECTION FOUR

Breaking Strongholds

For God has not given us a spirit of fear,
but of power, and of love, and of a sound mind.
(2 Timothy 1:7)

CHAPTER 12

Overcoming the Spirit of Fear

After a relaxing and very enjoyable honeymoon in the Cayman Islands, Benji and I settled into our new home in the Welsh Mountains of Narvon, Pennsylvania. I became a happy homemaker and continued the work I loved as an artist, painting anything from tee shirts and sweatshirts to children's furniture and craft items. Being busier than ever and no longer working at the tee shirt shop at Kitchen Kettle, I spent long and satisfying days building my own business and painting in the comfort and privacy of my new home.

Being married was like a dream to me. Benji and I are blessed to share a special closeness. We are truly compatible, and have always had a fun, relaxed relationship. I can be myself with Benji, not putting on airs or hiding anything. I've always been able to share my deepest and most private thoughts with him, even the really bad things. Amazingly, he still loves the person I am.

Reflecting back over the years, we have said many times that laughing together in the good times helped us get through the bad times. Both the fun and laughter in the carefree times and the closeness that comes with vulnerability and honesty in the hard times helped our relationship mature. And though Benji and I shared many common interests, we also pursued our own dreams and hobbies.

In the first several years, having a large and unkempt property to care for, we spent most of our Saturdays working outside. We enjoyed the long days outdoors and bantered in light conversation as we toiled side by side. They say the best things in life are free, and that certainly proved true for us.

After working up a sweat, on one particularly warm and humid Saturday afternoon, suddenly without warning the heavens opened in a torrent of rain. We ran through the pouring rain, getting soaked through and through. As Benji jogged ahead of me into the house, I lingered outside, lifting my face directly into the steady stream of rain. I was relishing the moment, enjoying the wild abandonment of common sense as the cool rain sent shivers through my body.

I didn't realize that my new husband was entertaining the malicious idea of locking me out of the house, leaving me standing outside on the brick doorstep in the rain. I should have seen it coming and quickly made a dash for the back door. Instead, I stupidly ran to the locked door and stood helplessly in the pouring rain, no longer enjoying its cool spray nearly as much.

Yelling and pounding on the door, I threatened to inflict all kinds of terrible pain on Benji, while he teasingly laughed at me from the warmth of the house. Suppressing laughter that was threatening to erupt, I glared darkly at him, sternly commanding him to open the door. But as my glistening, flashing brown eyes met his mischievous, greenish-brown eyes through the glass window of the locked door, I couldn't hide the wild and love-crazed passion I felt for him at that moment. My stern and rebuking demeanor reluctantly gave way to tenderness, and the pleasure was well worth the pain when my tormenter came back outside, wrapping his wet and dripping arms around me. The only sound heard was the sound of our laughter and the steady downpour of the rain, drenching us to the skin.

Maybe it was because I grew up with a house full of rowdy brothers who showed their love by picking on me, or maybe I just enjoy the attention. At any rate, Benji's teasing and the way he gets completely obnoxious at times has always been pleasurable and extremely funny to me. Even today, nothing makes me laugh louder or longer than when he's threatening to put me in some precarious situation, dropping his normally protective, sweet manner and turning into an obnoxious bully. This behavior, so out of his character, strikes me as hilarious.

We've always enjoyed spending a fair amount of time goofing off or whiling away many idle hours just sitting together and talking. However, the great amount of hard work in the first summer of our marriage kept us busy. We could only laughingly remember our dating days, when we had been so carefree. Because of the fact that we both enjoy the outdoors, sunshine and the water, we had spent countless Saturday afternoons together at the local public pool.

Soaking up the summer's warmth, we'd lounged and talked for hours; that is, when not trying to outdo each other on the diving board. Flaunting our expertise and bragging loudly about each fearless feat, we did flips, backward flips, dives, cannonballs, and anything else we could think of. But whoever did those things best paid later, being dunked and splashed unmercifully!

Our dating relationship had been fun and pleasant, with only a few bumps in the road. Knowing each other so well as close friends in the years before, we didn't have too many problems adapting to each other's ways. Of course, we had normal insecurities and doubts to work through as our trust in each other was building and becoming stronger.

During the fleeting months of dating, I had rarely spoken of the storms tossing to and fro beneath the surface of my emotions. There just was not a nice way of telling the love of my life, "Oh, by the way, behind my normally pleasant and sunny disposition is a wild and unpredictable streak of 'something awful' that does not even make sense to me." The strongholds that I struggled with daily had always been there—a few issues I just couldn't seem to overcome. But during our courtship, I had been successful most of the time in suppressing those deep inner conflicts.

Soon after marriage, it came as a surprise to Benji to behold the fun-loving, happy-go-lucky little gal he'd married having occasional meltdowns. Though I tried hard, I had never been able to get a handle on the deep anger that seemed to be smoldering just beneath the surface. It didn't happen every day or even every week, and there didn't seem to be any particular rhyme or reason for my outbursts. Something would trigger a spark within, and the fierce displays of wrath that came forth were astonishing.

It was impossible for Benji to understand my unprovoked rages when even I couldn't understand them. Besides, he was completely the opposite in his emotional makeup and always kept his cool. I did not know how to help my husband understand my radical behavior.

I had always had this problem, even as a child. I could become completely unglued and wild over the smallest problem. The simplest crisis, such as not being able to find something, was reason enough for a complete meltdown. At times, when I felt inadequate or very frustrated, my emotions became uncontrollable. Being determined, headstrong and impatient, I could not tolerate feeling victimized or helpless in any way. I hated when things went wrong. Never knowing how to overcome the unexpected bouts of anger, I just pushed the guilt and the dismal feelings of self-condemnation aside, allowing the problem to fester and grow through the years.

And it seemed the fear I'd always carried with me was also growing. As an adult, I thought I had learned to put my fears to rest. But then, like a caged animal set loose, they started tormenting me again, attempting to regain full control of my life.

I'd always hated sleeping alone in the darkness at night, and it had been a large source of anxiety for as long as I could remember. As a little girl, I slept fitfully, when I finally fell asleep. The gate leading to the large, open attic in the old farmhouse would creak and groan through the night, and I was convinced that someone was there waiting for me, waiting until I would be driven from my bed to go to the bathroom.

The only bathroom in the house was downstairs, and the trips down the long flight of stairs in the middle of the night filled me with terror. Knowing my brothers were close by in the rooms next to mine brought little comfort. Not realizing the depth or the reasons for my fear, the boys laughingly teased me, making me feel ashamed and needy.

I vowed not to let my fears show; but time and time again, I tip-toed silently to their bedsides in the middle of the night, begging one of them to go with me downstairs to use the bathroom. Whomever I could pull out of his warm cocoon would sigh loudly, mumbling unpleasantly under his breath.

Through the years, the fears came and went, getting worse for a while and then tapering off. Many things triggered them. It could have possibly been a story I heard, or a book I read. I had to be so careful what I allowed into my mind, avoiding anything even remotely scary. I had to protect myself from the flames of anxiety, or they would take over my senses, growing into a roaring fire that would devour me!

In the last few months before our marriage, for no apparent reason, my fears began to torment me again. Waking up in a sweat, I laid awake for hours alone in my apartment, fighting a losing battle with that inward sense of terror. I could hardly wait to be married. "I just need to hold out for a few short months," I kept telling myself. "Then I'll be able to escape the long, dark nights alone and will finally have someone to protect me."

So I was relieved when Benji and I moved into our new home together. For the first time in twenty-two years, I now had someone lying right beside me as I drifted off into dreamland. It felt wonderful to me, and I was overjoyed to leave the lonesome nights behind. Now, each night brought comfort and a deep, restful sleep. I felt so safe in the shelter of my husband's arms, at least for a short while.

Then, without warning, the nightmares started coming again. Beset by vicious anxiety attacks, the feelings of hopelessness came over me in waves. The clouds and shadows of darkness settled around me, suffocating and filling me with dread. Holding me close to him, Benji tried to comfort me, gently telling me, "Everything is okay." In the safety of his arms, the fear quickly disappeared.

But within the next several months, I began having panic attacks during the day. At home alone, for no apparent reason, I became terrified and experienced paralyzing fear and anxiety. Sobbing and gasping for air, I felt crippled and bound by the hysteria rising up inside while the fearful thoughts engulfed me!

Even when the attacks weren't happening, I carried the constant feelings of dread and uncertainty. The doors to my new home were always locked even during the day, and I worried fretfully that someone would enter our very private and sheltered property to harm me. When Benji was home, I loved our secluded home in the woods. But when he wasn't there, the thick brush and trees on all four sides of the house haunted me. There were no other houses nearby, and I felt unprotected and vulnerable. As the fears grew stronger and became more menacing, it seemed as if everything was spinning out of control. I could not understand what was happening to me.

I was also suffering from the chronic headaches that had always been frequent and unwelcome visitors in my life. The spasms in my jaw and neck became so painful at times that I wished to die. The headaches were always worse at night. The panic attacks were more threatening at night. I dreaded the darkness and dreaded sleeping. The physical pain combined with the phobias and panic attacks seemed unbearable, but I couldn't find a way to escape them.

Finally one night, while sensing oppression like never before, I was inconsolable. Visible only to me, there was a presence in the room, an overwhelming darkness that filled my spirit with riveting fear. I felt like I was suffocating as I tried to make sense of what was happening. Sobbing into Benji's chest, I choked out halting sentences, trying to explain the terror and anguish I felt. Benji, rocking me gently, was praying and asking God to help us. He suddenly felt compelled to ask me a strange question. "Have you ever gone through the steps of asking Jesus (out loud) to be the Lord of your life? Have you repented and renounced the sins of your past?"

I understood what Benji was saying: although I had always believed in Jesus and assumed I was a Christian, I couldn't remember ever consciously or audibly inviting Him into my heart. Of course, I had gone through the motions and done what I was told to do before my baptism, but it hadn't been very personal or meaningful to me. I had never really thought about asking God to cover my life with His protection and to wipe out the sins of my past.

Benji explained the importance of audibly asking Jesus Christ to be my Savior and the power there is in the confession and repentance of past sins. “By being intentional about truly making Jesus the Lord of your life, you will be making a statement—a statement of faith that will silence the doubts and fears in your own heart, while rendering the devil and his torment powerless. Then the light of God’s love will reign in your life, shielding you from the powers of darkness.”

With my husband’s encouragement, I went into the privacy of the bathroom; and meeting my Savior there, knelt and prayed my own prayer of repentance. Pouring out the depths of my heart, I asked Him to cleanse me from every ungodly act I had ever committed, naming the sins of my past as I remembered them, one by one. There were many, and I groaned and wept under the burden of them. I pleaded with Him to release me from the spirit of fear, and to give me peace. Urgently, in desperation, I surrendered all to God and His angels that night.

Hearing my own voice spoken into the silence of the night, I knew God could hear it too. His presence was immediate and strong, surrounding my body, comforting me. As I asked Jesus to come and reign in my heart and life, I could feel His Spirit penetrating my soul. It was a profound and enlightening experience, and one that I won’t forget. I never experienced a panic attack again. That was the night I embarked on the pathway to God’s forgiveness, love and renewal, seeking His perfect will for my life.

In the days and years that followed, my eyes were opened to so many things. I was able to clearly see how a little girl’s mind had been contaminated with filth and confusion. I now understood how quickly the effects of deep anxiety and fear, left unchecked, would have destroyed the plans of true victory God had for me. The warrior rose up within me, and I made a firm decision to follow after the things of God with all my heart, soul and mind. I developed a terrible hatred for the devil and his works of darkness. That night, I decided I was ready to start rejecting compromise and sin, and prepared to pursue a life of holiness, never turning back until I meet Jesus face to face.

All throughout my childhood, I thought it was normal to live in fear, constantly glancing over my shoulder. I was always on guard, clinging to the people around me, desperately terrified of being left alone. I did not realize until years later, how much the spirit of fear ruled my life. It seemed no one could relate to the gnawing feelings I struggled with daily, and I felt abandoned and alone. But now I know that my heavenly Father understands all of my emotions, and promises to be with me constantly, never leaving me or forsaking me. He tells me so, in many ways throughout His Word. I gain strength from these words in Deuteronomy 31:6a: *"Be strong, and of good courage, do not fear, nor be afraid of them; for the Lord your God, He is the One who goes with you."* Deuteronomy 31:8 is also powerful, when spoken with faith and confidence: *"And the Lord, He is the One who goes before you. He will be with you, He will not leave you or forsake you; do not fear, nor be dismayed."*

No matter what tactics the enemy will use against me, the promises in God's Word will always be my weapon. The spirit of fear is defeated in Jesus' name, as John 16:13a says: *"When He, the Spirit of Truth has come, He will guide you into all truth."* My mind is now filled with those truths.

When anxiety comes to smite my heart, I have a storehouse full of weapons of combat on which I can rely. It gives me confidence, and makes me feel powerful to hear the words from Psalms 91:10-11 roll off my lips: *"No evil shall befall you, nor shall any plague come near your dwelling; for He shall give His angels charge over you to keep you in all your ways."*

I know with a certainty that *"Greater is He"* that is in me *"than He that is in the world"* (1 John 4:4). I've experienced stumbling through the darkness in the lower realms of this world, but I've also had the pleasure of seeing the darkness flee as the light of God's protection and love moved into my spirit. Jesus Christ is the same yesterday, today and forever; His promises are just as powerful and real today as they were when God inspired their writing.

> *"Above all, taking the shield of faith, with which you will be able to quench all the fiery darts of the wicked one. And take the helmet of salvation, and the sword of the Spirit, which is the Word of God"* (Ephesians 6:16-17).

CHAPTER 13

Stepping into God's Plan

I had a new excitement for living, and wanted to find the real meaning and purpose for life. Although the fear continued to seize my mind, over time its grip diminished, little by little. The stronghold was beginning to fall. I knew the One who defeated all the world's anxieties and fears. I also knew with certainty that He was living inside of me. Because of that knowledge, I had new courage and strength to face each day.

The battle wasn't easy, and the fight in me continued for many years. Knowing that true peace was rightfully mine as a child of God, I fought hard with everything in me. Even so, the progress was slow and painful. I experienced the extreme difficulty of tearing down strongholds that had been reared in me since early childhood.

With every step in the right direction, and with each day of more healing and deliverance, I developed a stronger desire to somehow bring light to a darkened world. Experiencing deliverance through the power of Jesus Christ made me realize that I had something valuable to give to others. I knew many people who needed Jesus in a personal way.

There was a dream taking shape in my heart. Having always been passionate about singing, I started envisioning the possibility of sharing God's redeeming love and power through music. I'd always wanted to sing publicly, ever since playing the piano in that restaurant with my parents at six years of age. My desire to play music and sing grew stronger with every passing year, until it became irresistible. I prayed for a way to use my gift of music.

On a cold winter evening, Benji and I went to yet another hockey game at the Lancaster rink. He competed in vigorous games of ice hockey several times a week, and I usually tagged along to watch the games. On that particular evening, I was sitting on the cold bleachers after the game awaiting my new husband. He was in the locker room with about twenty other ambitious and smelly hockey players, getting showered and dressed for the drive home.

As I sat there shivering, a guy I didn't know very well approached me. Manny Lapp and I were not close friends, just acquaintances. After the initial "Hello," Manny got right to the point. He was starting a band with two other guys. He had heard about my love of music and asked if I would consider trying out for lead and background singing with the band.

Well, I nearly leapt off the bleachers in my excitement, shooting questions at him faster than he could answer. No longer shivering or cold, I was ecstatic. Grinning calmly in his quiet way, he answered my fiery questions, being sure to tell me that there was not much organization or direction in the band yet. "We hope to perform in the public eye someday. But, if it doesn't happen, it's no big deal. It's just something we're playing around with."

So after much discussion with Benji, we agreed that being in a band would be a great project to take on. The next Tuesday evening I was at Manny's house, in the basement, where their sound system was set up. Along with Manny, who played electric guitar, there was Nate King on bass guitar. I didn't know him very well either, but had seen him around town. Then there was Mark Stoltzfus, the drummer, whom I had never met.

We talked for a long while, sharing the history and experience in music we had. Of course, I didn't have much to tell. I'd played keyboard and had always sung at home. My friend Sally and I had played and sung together quite a few times for small crowds, but that was all I had to say for myself. Nate King had never played anywhere in particular either; just here and there with a few guys on occasion. The story was the same for the drummer, Mark.

Manny, on the other hand, had been involved musically for a good while. He told us about the many places he'd performed with a rock band, for several years. Admittedly, they were only a small local band that played in bars, but we were impressed that he'd actually been with an established band that was known in the area.

Since becoming a Christian, Manny wanted to play music that would have a positive message. Although his former band was still going strong, he had opted out, wanting to start something better. So there we were: four inexperienced musicians who had little to offer each other except big dreams.

That first evening, we just jammed. Manny was right when he said there was no organization or direction. There were song lyrics scattered everywhere, a crazy mixture of country, rock and Gospel tunes. We played them all, in no particular order. One minute we were serenely singing the hymn, "Jesus Signed My Pardon," and the next, Nate was crooning the song "Lyin' Eyes." Then we'd lurch into a string of country tunes, only to return to heart-stirring songs about God, love and heaven a few minutes later.

Finally, I said, “Stop the music, and let’s talk.” In disbelief, I asked, “Is this what you do every practice, play this unusual mix of songs?” Looking around the circle, I had to smile. As guys go, these were no exceptions.

Mark, sitting in the darkened corner behind the drums grinned sheepishly and said, “Yeah, what’s wrong with that?”

Nate quickly added, “We’re just jamming, and these are the songs we know.”

Manny just grinned from his perch on the Coors Light Beer® stool he was sitting on, the one thing he hadn’t parted with from the previous band.

Next, I stated the obvious, “If we hope to go anywhere at all, we’ll need to pick one particular genre of music, and stick with it.” Next I asked them which venues, if we got publicity, would they would want to play. They weren’t sure. They seemed to be pretty sure about wanting to play secular country music; but the longer we talked, the more we were coming to the conclusion that country Gospel music would be better for us, because we felt that would draw more people to listen to our music. In a self-serving way, we were clearly looking out for our own interests. Based on that reasoning we made the decision to play country Gospel music, hoping to play at church functions and other Christian events.

Having squared that away, we could get on with practice. We played every Gospel song we could think of, rejoicing if they sounded good and throwing them out if they didn’t. I was excited, to say the least. That was the most fun I’d had doing music in all of my life. Needless to say, I was thrilled and relieved when at the end of the evening, the guys invited me back the following week.

As I was leaving, I picked up each and every song sheet lying around on the floor. Flinging them onto a large pile, I sternly declared that I'd be taking them with me. "I will return with them next week in a nice, organized fashion, within the confines of four black folders."

The guys just laughed at me and shrugged their shoulders: "Fine with us. Suit yourself."

It wasn't long until we had a complete band, adding Roman Lapp, who played lead and rhythm electric guitar. Soon after that, Rebecca Stoltzfus joined the band as well to help out with background vocals. Knowing we needed to find a name for the band, we put our heads together, trying to come up with something agreeable to all of us. For several weeks, we threw around the possibilities of many different names, but each one came out sounding awkward and weird, reducing us to much laughter. Our best efforts to name the band were hilarious.

To our surprise, Nate sauntered into practice one evening and announced nonchalantly, "Hey guys, how do you all feel about the name "Breakthrough"? Everybody turned and stared at him, bringing their senseless chatter to an abrupt halt. The sudden silence in the room was quickly disrupted by yelps and shouts of agreement. "Breakthrough" was simple, strong and meaningful—but powerful. Yes, that was it! Yes! We had a name!

We were astounded when just a few months later we were invited to play at the Haiti Sale, a large annual event to raise money for the poverty-stricken people of Haiti. Nervously approaching the stage on the evening of our very first concert, we plugged away through all of our songs and were rewarded with exuberant applause from the audience.

The most amusing thing happened that evening and seemed to help break the ice because it made everyone laugh.

As we were singing the song, "It's Raining," the clouds overhead darkened, and the heavens suddenly opened, pouring down buckets of rain on our tent. Everyone rushed under cover, and we all laughed uproariously when we realized what we were singing. For years, people remembered the night Breakthrough sang "It's Raining" and "made it rain."

Shortly after the Haiti sale, we were asked to sing at a local seven day event, a revival tent meeting in New Holland, Pennsylvania. We politely turned it down, saying we were not ready for something that big, as we didn't know our songs very well. But the folks booking the revival insisted and wouldn't take "No" for an answer.

So our second appearance turned out to be a stretching experience for all of us. Feeling like baby birds that had been pushed out of the nest, we stumbled into the week, not knowing what to expect. As the people poured in every evening, we struggled to keep our end up musically. Feeling very inexperienced, we'd gone from never playing in public to suddenly playing every evening.

I was also struggling in a different way that week. Although I felt I had a good relationship with the Lord and knew He loved me, I continued to struggle with being a truly "good" person. It seemed there were always the churning feelings of unrest in my spirit that I couldn't put away. No matter how hard I tried, no matter how much I wanted to be good, the rebellion inside always seemed to win.

There were so many things I couldn't get a handle on—the bad language, my bad attitude, my out-of-control temper, bitterness toward other people. Most peculiarly, I held a strong dislike and wariness for those who really were good people. I thought they were proud and stuffy, and I resented them.

There were many mixed emotions swirling within me as I stood on the platform night after night. We played for about forty-five minutes every evening. Then we listened to the fiery sermons the minister preached. After the altar call, we returned to the stage to sing an invitational hymn. As we sang, "Just as I Am" or "Have Thine Own Way," the preacher appealed to the crowd of people to come forward and accept Christ as their Savior, making Him the Lord and Redeemer of their lives. As people came weeping and knelt at the altar, I watched in amazement. I couldn't imagine the boldness it would take to openly display the sinful state of your soul and feel such passion and emotion in front of all of those people.

I wondered why I felt so cold inside and so untouched. I loved the Lord. I really did. I watched the people who were repenting and wanted to feel those strong emotions that were so obviously having such a powerful effect on them. But as usual, I just felt numb inside and saw no hope of that ever changing. Pushing it out of my mind, I chose not to think about it too much.

The end of the week came, and the minister and the revival committee decided to prolong the revival meetings because there were so many people repenting every evening. Nobody wanted to stop the flow of God's Spirit at work, so we continued into the ninth evening before the meetings were over.

It had been a wonderful week for many people. I enjoyed the revival, but the people that repented barely even registered in my mind. My strongest memories were the songs and music we played as a band, and the fun we'd had.

In all honesty, we could hardly wait until the meetings were over, because we had a beach trip planned on the following weekend. For the band, it was all about having fun, and there was seldom a serious moment in the first year we performed together.

But time moved on. God's plan for us was about to unfold in a series of exciting and unusual events. In the next seven years, although there were many strongholds coming down in my own life, I was used by God to minister to others through singing, prayer and mostly love.

There wasn't a course of training available that could show me how to love people or care about their pain. However, nobody had to teach me how to connect with the ones who were hurting. As I experienced more and more of God's mercy in my own life, my heart ached for other people I knew were hurting, and I became concerned and compassionate. The internal battles I was still fighting gave me incredible love and empathy for people who were carrying heavy burdens, who needed a listening ear. I knew the power of a simple prayer because of the effect of other people's prayers for me in the past. So I was able to come confidently before God's throne on behalf of the girls and women we met. I knew this would touch their lives in the same way that godly people had helped me.

Something inside kept urging me to reach out and make a difference in the world. I learned that God is no respecter of persons, and it doesn't matter how long we've been serving Him or how small or insignificant we feel. He needs us to be His hands and feet, to reach out to the people who come into our lives. I felt the call on my life and answered it to the best of my ability at the time.

Music became my outlet. Almost immediately after Manny, Nate, Mark and I met to start the band, I started writing songs for the group. I've always had a special love for poetry. As soon as I knew how to form words and sentences in school, I started making them rhyme. As I attempted to put songs together for the band, the lyrics and melody lines came together effortlessly. Day after day, I worked on writing and composing songs. I composed from those secret chambers in my heart that understood the wounded and the broken.

I also arranged music as means of offering praise and thankfulness to God. The songs in my heart, written from the deep abyss of many lonesome, trembling and passionate moments, became my voice. Added to that, my love for the old hymns I sang as a child never left me; I knew I would always include some of them in every program as well.

Despite much imperfection and the lack of professional training, we established a reputation and started playing throughout Pennsylvania and several surrounding states. After Kevin Sensenig joined the band, bringing his lively keyboard skills into the group, we had a total of five instruments on stage: a keyboard, two electric guitars, a bass guitar and drums. Adding the vocalists, we had seven people in the group for several years. Later, Nate King's new bride, Joanna, joined us as well, making it eight. My husband Benji was our financial manager and ran sound for the band from the day we started.

Together, with the rest of the group, we set off for new adventures, becoming well-known in Ohio, Indiana, Illinois, Missouri, Iowa, and even Canada. We also did lots of local gigs at town events, festivals, fund-raisers and churches.

We became more excited about ministry as time went on. The phone calls we received made us realize the effect our music was having on people's lives. Women I'd never met from other states called just to thank me for our music. They often shared their stories with me. Often they were sad stories of brokenness, disappointment, rejection or mistreatment. It has truly been rewarding to know that people have found comfort and healing in the lyrics of our songs.

A rejoicing mother gave me a call one evening and thanked me over and over for our music, telling me that her sons, who would never listen to Christian music before, were now listening to our CDs. I rejoiced with her as I felt the concern she had for her precious sons' souls.

Our band began having occasional altar calls after concerts. These were never planned beforehand. However, as we were nearing the end of our set, I would sometimes feel a strange but strong prompting to extend an invitation urging those who wanted to accept Jesus to come forward. All I needed to do was have a few hushed words with Nate, who usually stood right next to me, and he would quickly nod his head in agreement, always completely open to what the Holy Spirit was doing.

On one such evening, the band was playing in an open field, set up on an old farm wagon. Hundreds of people had come out for the beautiful summer evening, bringing lawn chairs and blankets. It was a quiet, peaceful evening. As the sun went down, my heart became burdened and filled with burning desire to see God glorified and to see lives changed; I knew the time was right for an altar call.

As we sang the last song of the evening, an upbeat favorite that everyone knew very well, the crowd was brimming with excitement. Wild cheers went up as we finished with a final drum roll. Then, THUD... and there was silence.

Giving Nate "the look," I spoke into the night, hesitantly at first, my voice getting stronger as the passion within me rose. My voice broke as I shared some of my own life's experiences, and the sin that kept me bound for so many years. I also spoke of God's power to change everything and how He came to live on the inside, bringing cleansing, renewal and peace.

With a simple invitation, we sang another song. As we sang, out of the shadows came one, then two, then three and four... more and more young teenage boys came to kneel in the sharp stubble of hay in front of the wagon where we were standing, until there was a total of fifteen. Yes, fifteen young souls found Jesus that night.

As older men came out of the crowd to pray with each one of them, I felt a curious mixture of emotions that is hard to describe. The scene was strangely beautiful. There was the darkness of the summer night, the sunset in the distance, and the large hay field looming out to meet the twilight. We stood on the old, scruffy farm wagon with the harsh glare of the spotlight streaming down on us. Fifteen repentant boys were kneeling on the ground with fathers and older men admonishing and encouraging them.

I'll never forget that moment or its purity. God's power became real to me, and I could feel His deep compassion and mercy for all who called on Him. It touched me in a profound way, and I felt an urgent desire to see Him move in more people's lives.

CHAPTER 14

Africa

Throwing our lives into the band, Benji and I became excited about the potential the group had for music ministry. Normal life went on, but my mind was consumed with plans and ideas for the future. Reaching out to hurting people who came into my life, offering a listening ear or a simple prayer and giving comfort to those experiencing emotional turmoil became my driving force.

The entire band worked together with renewed energy. Through Kevin, our keyboard player, we got to know Titus Mbai. Titus was very passionate about sharing the Gospel message. He was an evangelistic preacher who pastored several large churches in Kenya, Africa. On his visits to America, Titus always spent a lot of time at Kevin and Sherry Sensenig's house. It didn't take long before Titus Mbai heard about the band Kevin had joined, the band called "Breakthrough."

As we got to know Titus better, all of the band members enjoyed hearing his many stories about life and ministry in Africa. However, we were completely unprepared when he casually invited us to come to Kenya to sing. Laughing, I'd said, "Right, Titus. The Kenyans wouldn't even understand the words we're singing, so how could we possibly minister to them?"

To our surprise, he said, "English is indeed the second language in our region of Africa. Most Kenyans understand and speak English fluently. I want you to come, all of you. I think it will be a wonderful experience for the African people and for the whole band."

To say that our band was a high-spirited, ambitious group was an understatement. We loved adventure and going to new places, but the thought of going to Africa was more than we could imagine! Oh, the sheer craziness of it seemed so exciting and we all knew we wanted to go. It didn't take us long to make the decision. Yes, we would go to Kenya, Africa in August, just a few short months away. We would also raise the money we needed for plane tickets through concerts and fund-raisers during the upcoming summer.

Titus told us we would need around $25,000 for the three-week trip. So we launched into a very busy summer of concerts. I don't recall turning any concerts down that summer. Every call that came in was met with an exuberant, "Yes, give me the time and place, and we'll be there!" So we were playing all over Lancaster County, at every backyard party, town function, festival or church that would have us.

We rarely asked to be paid, but at each concert we let people know that we were going to Africa in a few months and needed as much money as they could give. We were astounded by everyone's generosity. Being greatly encouraged, we kept plowing through the full summer schedule of concerts. As the months flew by, we kept getting more and more money, which Benji carefully deposited into our "Africa Fund" that he'd set up at the local bank.

A few short months later, thanks to many people's amazing generosity, we had managed to raise a total of $24,090.00. We knew the hand of God was in this journey, and all of the band members were awed by the swiftness of His outpoured blessings.

With great excitement and high spirits, we embarked on a journey that would take us around the world, but what awaited us there was something we could not have imagined. The extreme poverty we beheld was overwhelming. The emptiness we saw in the eyes of children wandering alone and unprotected on the streets was disheartening and sad. I knew right from the first second we arrived in Kenya that my time on this continent would change my life.

They had church services every day in the morning, which we often attended. Several times one of the members of our group would preach the message for the day, which we found to be very interesting. Then the afternoons were spent setting up our sound system, getting ready for the revival meetings, which were held almost every evening during our three-week stay in Kenya.

After setting up a stage on the edge of town out in the middle of an open field, we started playing in the evenings around 6:00 pm. There were always lots of people there before we started playing, but as the music carried far into the night, more and more people from town appeared in the open field. By service time, there were hundreds of spectators.

It was never long before the people were clapping and swaying to the music, and it seemed the whole crowd was moving in unison. Not afraid to show their emotions, they shouted, danced and held their hands high. Sometimes the people waved their arms frantically while their eyes were tightly closed, as if desperately trying to get God's attention. Even the smallest of the children danced and clapped joyously to the music.

Then there were fiery messages preached as we left the stage, joining the crowd of onlookers. Amazed by the passion and excitement with which Titus Mbai, Randy Martin and the others preached, I listened and observed. Each evening ended with an altar call, when many people surrendered their lives to God. Of course, there was always prayer for the sick as well.

It seemed as if salvation and physical healing went hand in hand in Kenya. I was vividly interested, intensely curious, yet a little doubtful, as I heard their prayers and the numerous testimonies that people were being miraculously healed of various infirmities and health problems. I had conflicting thoughts on this subject and wasn't sure how I felt about it. I certainly did believe God was capable of healing, and I believed that the soul and the body connection was inseparable. But having seen so many unanswered prayers concerning physical healing, including my own, I wasn't so sure God would really heal the sick on such a large scale.

One evening, a man in a wheelchair clumsily rolled himself into the crowd. Eagerly, I watched him and hoped he'd be healed so that I could witness an undeniable miracle. As I stared at him, I could just imagine it: after a heartfelt prayer for healing, the man would suddenly stand up and fling his wheelchair aside. He would walk victoriously across the stage while the crowd cheered for him.

But I was disappointed as night after night he returned to listen intently to the fiery messages that were preached, but remained at a distance. Staying on the outskirts of the crowd, he never ventured close to the stage or made any effort to speak with anyone. He seemed content to be bound to that wheelchair forever, which greatly troubled me. I became agitated because he wouldn't go forward for prayer when the invitation was extended. A part of me wanted to go over to him, grab the handles of his wheelchair and shove him closer to that stage myself. But it really wasn't just for his sake that I wanted his healing so badly. It was for mine as well. My faith in God seemed weak and shallow at the time. I just wanted to see something great and amazing, thinking that would help my faith in God grow and come alive. I needed answers to the questions clouding my mind.

Some of the people from our team did see quite a few miraculous healings. There was one miracle in particular that stood out to everyone, especially the persons who observed it. A woman who was blind in one eye approached the stage and asked for prayer for healing. Her damaged eye didn't have a pupil and was completely white. As the people surrounding her laid hands on her and prayed, they watched in amazement as the brown part of her eye came in and her missing pupil appeared perfect and normal. For the first time in many years the woman could see out of both eyes!

I should have been happy, even rejoicing, as my friends told and retold the story; but I hadn't seen it for myself, so it really didn't excite me much. The old, dissatisfying, spiritual numbness had found me again, even there in the plains of Africa. This doubting spirit was preventing me from seeing the full glory of God's great power, even though I was privileged to be so close to its manifestation.

As the weeks went on, I grew weary of the meetings, and wished I weren't involved in the revivals at all. After we were finished with the music each evening, I became lost in my own thoughts, trying to sort them out. I wondered why I couldn't feel the passion these simple, impoverished folks obviously felt, when I had so much to be thankful for and they had so little. Quietly watching everyone around me, I shrank back, trying to become as an invisible form, and pretending I wasn't really there.

My curiosity was aroused by the loud, "in-your-face" style of preaching. The people's responses pleased me tremendously and were entertaining to watch. There certainly was not a dull moment there. I enjoyed watching the sudden shouts of agreement to the preached Word and the constant noise of the crowd. Why wasn't I more excited? Why did I feel as if I had nothing to offer these people? Was I not equipped to deal with spirituality on this level? My mind was full of doubts that taunted me. As the sun went down in the African skies and the shadows of darkness clouded its light, the recurring questions and doubts also clouded my mind.

Later, back at the motel where we were staying, my spirit came alive once again as we released pent-up energy with a vigorous and exuberant pillow fight. It felt so good to pound my fellow band-members with the overstuffed, fat, white pillows, while simultaneously dodging the pillows coming swiftly toward me. Gasping for air and laughing hysterically, we caused quite a ruckus that night. We'd always had lots of fun together as a band, on or off stage. Whether we were all talking at once over dinner, watching videos and munching on snacks, or just doing nothing, we always had a good time. The humor ran high, and everyone peppered the conversation with heavy doses of sarcasm and wit.

As the week progressed, aside from the tiredness that seemed to follow me and despite my wandering and sometimes troubling thoughts, I thoroughly enjoyed every day. I loved going to the simple but neat homes of people in the church. They were fun to be around and always seemed happy and eager to serve us the best food they had to give.

The food in Kenya was delicious. We ate most of the foods they served us, only passing up some of the more peculiar-looking dishes. The highlight on our "missionary menu" was the tasty, melt-in-your-mouth barbecued goat meat we enjoyed one evening. Juicy and tender, it had been slowly cooked over a roaring bonfire outside.

I also loved playing with the children. They clutched tightly to our hands and crowded around us, touching our hair when they could get close enough. I was drawn to their sweet innocence, and I was touched by the love they so freely gave.

It was a wonderful experience to be able to help teach the children's Sunday School class at church on a beautiful Sunday morning. The large class was assembled outside the church on the rolling yard. While Sherry Sensenig told the story of "Noah and the Ark," I drew pictures of it on a chalkboard that was set up on the walkway. The children watched and listened in delight, their dark eyes shining. When the class was dismissed, each child shook our hands and thanked us. They were all so very precious.

I loved the peacefulness and simplicity that I found in the people. Compared to the fast-paced life we normally lived, a slow-paced life was a welcomed change. My mind seemed to be catching up with my emotions, and things were becoming clearer as time went on.

As the weeks wore on, it didn't seem to matter as much that I didn't always feel completely exuberant and wildly passionate about the things of God. It no longer seemed as important to understand everything so clearly, because the contentment in my heart was growing deeper every day. God's Spirit was telling me that it was okay just to be me, assuring me that whatever stage of life I was in at the time was right where I was meant to be at that point in my journey. He wasn't asking for more than I could give but was accepting what little I had to offer.

Back in America again three weeks later, we arrived at the airport where several of the band members' families eagerly awaited us. Driving the remainder of the way home in a large, fifteen-passenger van, we were exhausted, but happy. It had been a good trip, a growing and learning experience for all of us.

The thing that was so amazing about the whole surreal experience was how God met our financial need. At the end of the trip we had exactly twenty-five dollars left over. That was all that was left of the thousands of dollars we'd raised. Who would have thought that it would end up so close to zero? Not much money was left over, but it was just enough. Once again, we had experienced the never-failing provision and blessings of God.

CHAPTER 15

Restoration

Several years later, at the age of twenty-eight, I had to admit to myself that I wasn't experiencing the true victory that I knew should be available "in Christ." Even though there were many exciting things happening with the band, the strongholds in my life were only becoming more apparent as time went on. Not that other people could see; even some of my closest friends didn't know of my inner conflicts.

Although I was no longer experiencing the terrible, debilitating panic attacks, the fear continued to plague me. Worse than anything were the extreme bouts of anger that erupted repeatedly and without warning, leaving me feeling discouraged and disappointed in myself. I could no longer deny the "other" part of me that often left me feeling so unsettled. The coldness, arrogance and restlessness I felt, along with my cynical approach to life, didn't seem to line up with true Christianity.

Not realizing that childhood victimization and abuse negatively affect a person's whole range of emotions, I became self-deprecating, dismally berating myself for the weaknesses I couldn't overcome. Not knowing why I couldn't control my emotions, nor knowing how to deal with the negativity in my mind, I knew I needed answers to the questions that still haunted me.

While bravely continuing with the band, my personal life was in turmoil. I sought the counsel of a Christian woman who is a professional, Spirit-filled therapist, to help me in the cleansing and renewing of my mind. Throughout the course of the next year, I met with her regularly. With insight and compassion, she walked with me through the shadows of my past.

During the first or second visit, she told me it would possibly help to bring closure and healing to my heart and mind if I wrote my inner feelings down on paper. They would not be for anyone to read, but my private thoughts would stir up memories that I needed to conquer.

I eagerly got started the next day, but found I could not put my feelings into words. My writing was stiff and unfeeling, not connecting with my emotions, and I became very frustrated. Then I remembered the many, many poems I had written ever since I could spell, and how my thoughts and words came together so well in poetry. I started writing, and the floodgates opened.

The words poured out of me faster than I could write, and the tears flowed freely as well. I penned it all in a very short time, swiftly and surely. As I'd done countless times before, I turned to God. But it was different this time. Seeing my words written on the white notebook paper made me become more aware of the harsh reality of my early life. With every stroke of the pen, I committed more fully to the emotions I was carrying, no longer being able to deny them and the deep pain they brought.

When finished, I no longer saw the little girl in the shadows of my past as a stranger, or as some other person who was vague and unreal, as I'd always done before. For the first time in my life, I became one with her, the child deep within me who had been so alone and so afraid in those times. In my mind I embraced her and held her close, comforting her. I found myself identifying completely with her. The numbness I had used to cover my emotions was ripped away, as the depth of the pain, misunderstandings and confusion wracked my body and spirit. Although coming face to face with the ghosts in my past was almost more than I could bear, ironically, it made me feel more alive than ever before.

As many others have before, I discovered that the first step to inner healing is being able to feel the pain. The act of writing my scattered thoughts down on paper opened those doors that had been held tightly closed for most of my early life.

I knew there could be no real completion to the poem, because there were too many questions still persisting in my mind that seemingly had no answers. With mixed emotions and a heavy heart, I drew my writings to a close with a plea to my Lord, asking Him to fight and win the battle that was still raging in my soul, and to loose the chains that held me bound.

I haven't shared this poem with anyone, except my husband and my mother. It bares the heart of a grown woman who was soon to give birth to her first child, while still trying to make sense of her own childhood. I never put a title on my poem. I didn't consider the verses to be profound or worthy of a title or a name. They were just words, written from my heart that helped me process and bring to light the hidden, scattered fragments of information that had been pushed to the back of my mind for so many years....

My God, my God, I'm here today
So many things I have to say;
So many questions in my mind,
So many memories of days gone by...

You know the story of my life,
The smiles, the laughter, and the tears I cried.
You know all that I'm made of,
You know, my Lord, I need Your love.

I came into the world, so small
So vulnerable to it all,
So trusting, so sensitive and sweet,
No torment or fear, my mind was free.

I rested in Your love each day,
The sun shone down where I lay
So helpless and frail, but I knew no fear.
My cries brought comfort to wipe my tears.

I blossomed and grew, surrounded by love
And blessings flowed down from above;
Safe and secure with my family,
Your hand of love protecting me.

But then so quickly, it was snatched away.
My world was shattered on that day!
Innocence gone, I learned to fear
But no one was there to wipe my tears.

The questions were swimming in my mind,
Confusion took over my young life.
My vision grew dim, dreams were pushed back,
And the secret thoughts were all I had.

The constant fear I could not hide
So I pushed those thoughts all aside;
The deeper I pushed the more ingrained
In my troubled mind they became.

I didn't know these memories would burn
In my mind, waiting to return,
Waiting to torment my wounded heart,
Waiting to tear my emotions apart.

But life went on, the future looked bright.
I thought my darkness had turned to light.
I thought my mind had erased
The sadness, as if I'd never faced.

I threw all caution to the wind,
Allowing sin to enter in,
Through the door I'd opened wide,
Oh, I flung my cares all aside.

But now I carried new concerns,
My life had taken another turn.
I now could feel the Lord's rebuke
As His ways I forsook.

Traveling down the sinful path,
I could feel the sting of God's wrath.
But, oh my heart hungered so,
To my desires, I couldn't say "No."

Before I had feared the hands of men
And running was my best defense.
But as I faced the judgments in His word,
Now I feared the hands of God.

Nowhere to run, and nowhere to hide,
Before my Savior I knelt and cried...
I cried my sorrows, pain and grief
And I laid them there at His feet.

Surely my troubles were left behind,
True peace and happiness would now be mine.
My hopes and dreams would fall in place
And the past I would never have to face.

Now I'm here today, blessed with so much,
Hand in hand with the man I love.
The good in life I do see
And a part of me is so happy and free.

So Lord, I'm asking, why the fear?
Why does the torment reappear?
Will I ever be free of pain?
And will I ever be whole again?

I want to have faith, believe in Your name,
To know that I'm safe, without blame!
I wonder, I fear, I fret, and I ask,
Is Heaven within my lowly grasp?

Is it enough, what I have to give?
Or do you need more, my Lord above?
I gave you my heart, and soul bare,
I'll give you my life, and all my cares.

So Lord, I ask that You speak to my heart;
Show me the way, and I'll do my part.
Open my eyes to see the truth,
Guide my steps to follow You.

Let me see the good in life,
Let my mind be free of pain and strife.
I pray for healing from the inside out,
That Your goodness I never again will doubt.

Cleanse my mind from the fears therein.
Oh Lord, don't let the enemy win!
The battle belongs to You, my God.
Put all life's given me under the blood.

Take these chains that hold me bound;
Lift the weights that pull me down.
Loose the prison bars around me;
And let Your arms of love surround me.

I felt many mixed emotions concerning the poem and couldn't bring myself to show it to anyone for years. In many ways it shamed me. I hated to expose the confusion in my mind, and didn't like the way the weakness and vulnerability felt. Much preferring to stay hidden behind the smiling face and confidence that I portrayed so well, I kept the dark blue notebook containing the poem hidden away. For many years, it lay at the bottom of a drawer, buried under some clothes.

However, writing it had opened new doors for me. In my personal thoughts and musings, I was leaping and running through those doors, experiencing the mighty healing that comes when a person's soul lies open before God. I cried buckets of tears as I found answers to the questions that had persisted in my mind for years. The reasons for my dysfunctions were exposed, and things began to make sense to me as my counselor patiently unraveled the frayed edges of my past. This "unraveling" brought a sense of purpose and hope for the future.

With my counselor's help and gentle guidance, God's promises and words of truth became medicine to my heart, soul and emotions. Breaking the curse of destruction on my life, I received all that God had for me, claiming the promises placed throughout the Bible. As I built my future on His promises, a ray of light began to penetrate the darkness within, bringing healing to my spirit. It was an intense period of time as I faced the demons within, freeing myself of their power. Some things were easy to let go of, but many of the strongholds that had gotten their grip on me didn't seem willing to let go without a struggle. My mind became a battleground between the forces of good and evil as the walls came down.

The verses in James 4:7-8a became real and meaningful to me, and I gained strength from pondering those few simple, yet powerful words: *"Therefore submit to God. Resist the devil and he will flee from you. Draw near to God, and He will draw near to you."* And as I did draw near to God, He gave me the strength to resist the devil and the deceptions that had been planted in my mind.

The oppression I'd been under for so many years gave way to God's deliverance and peace of mind, as His Spirit filled the cavities of my soul: *"The Lord also will be a refuge for the oppressed, a refuge in times of trouble. And those who know Your name will put their trust in You; for You, Lord, have not forsaken those who seek You"* (Psalms 9: 9-10).

I grew closer to God with each passing day, as I felt his love and mercy being poured out like water to quench my thirst. Now it was easy to freely accept God's forgiveness and restoration. For several years, I felt as if my arms were constantly extended, outstretched to my Savior, just drinking in and receiving everything good He had for me. As He supplied me with the weapons of truth and light, exposing and stripping away the power of deception, my mind became clear and my resolve firm and sure.

CHAPTER 16

Controlled by the Spirit

I've always had an intense fascination for the spirit world and the spiritual part of human beings. Amazingly, our spirits have the ability to connect with the Spirit of Almighty God! But we also have the ability to connect with evil spirits (demonic powers), which will quickly bring confusion and oppression to our lives. That is why it's so important to ask the Holy Spirit of God to reign in our lives. We need His Spirit within us if we want to bear good fruit and lead a positive life of victory: *"The fruit of the Spirit is love, joy, peace, longsuffering, kindness, goodness, faithfulness, gentleness, self-control...."* (Galatians 5:22-23). Our lives will only produce an abundance of these fruits if God's Spirit is within us.

The opposites of the fruit of the Spirit are anger, hatred, jealousy, pride, depression and unforgiveness. If any one of these negative emotions takes root in us, we will desperately need the Spirit of God to overcome it. We have to lean heavily on His guidance to lead the way to freedom and deliverance. This may be a long and difficult journey. If there are strongholds that have been left unchecked for many years, it may also take years to be released from them.

One of the most tenacious strongholds in my life has been the spirit of anger. In the dictionary, anger is described as "distress or a feeling of displeasure and hostility because of being injured, mistreated or opposed." I believe there are appropriate times for anger, and to simply feel the emotion of anger may not be wrong. Sometimes God will put a righteous anger inside of us to stir up our spirits, preparing us for battle against the things that displease Him. However, anger should quickly dissipate, and should be replaced with prayer and action, according to the Spirit's leading. It is the way we react to anger that makes it right or wrong, and we especially need the Holy Spirit's leading in heated moments.

To harbor hatred or to lash out in violence because of deep seated anger is wrong and displeasing to God. The latter has often plagued me. Anger has been a huge source of discouragement to me, many times causing me to spin into deep despair. I've struggled with bouts of anger since childhood, and I haven't been taught to control it very well, so it felt natural for me to give in to this spirit.

When I get too caught up in the busy activities of everyday life and push God aside, I become more prone to losing my temper. If I do not stay rooted and grounded in God's Word, I often find myself coming into agreement with this demonically inspired attitude, allowing anger to take over my better judgment. That is why the verses in John 15:4-5 are so meaningful to me, a powerful passage in which Jesus confides: *"Abide in Me, and I in you. As the branch cannot bear fruit of itself, unless it abides in the vine, neither can you, unless you abide in Me. I am the vine, you are the branches. He who abides in Me, and I in him, bears much fruit; for without Me, you can do nothing."*

When a branch is cut off the vine, which is its life-giving source, that branch won't live longer than a few days. It will soon wither and die. I believe the very same thing happens to us spiritually if we don't stay closely connected to God on a daily basis. Weakness occurs with separation from the Spirit of God. As I've experienced, there are grave consequences for yielding to anger and not staying connected to God.

As a mother of four children, and also being involved in a music ministry, I feel I am doing what God has called me to do. I enjoy being faithful to the duties and callings in my life; but having a full and demanding schedule with many different responsibilities, I must admit that I can quickly become overwhelmed and uptight. While I am actually getting into the swing of things and learning to enjoy the excitement of the journey, one thing that can be frustrating to me is having less quiet time to nurture my own spirit. I usually spend these 'alone times' reading. I have always been passionate about studying literature that covers a variety of subjects. In the last decade, I have also come to especially love the Bible, realizing it is spiritually alive. I enjoy meditating on the words in this book because they hold tremendous power for my journey through this world. However, setting aside enough time for this can be challenging.

There was a certain point in my life when I began to feel exceedingly overwhelmed and busy. Each day passed by so fast. I felt that I had no time for mind renewal or time with God. Just as a flower, cut from the plant, appears to thrive for a while, I also appeared to be doing just fine. But just as the flower begins to droop and wither after a few days, my soul started languishing. I knew in my heart that I had been drifting away from God, but couldn't seem to find the desire or strength to make the changes that were necessary.

Over time, pressure began building up inside me. Without warning, everything started crumbling down, all within a few days. My moods began going up and down like a yo-yo, and I shut out the whole world, including my husband. Benji and I were constantly arguing about some silly thing or another, and I had very little patience with my four darling daughters. Even our large Mastiff dog, Tracy, got a kick or complaint from me in passing. Normally having much love and compassion for other people, I was alarmed by my coldness and lack of sympathy.

The girls couldn't figure out what had gotten into their mother who was usually so tender, warm and loving. Benji was thinking a quiet, peaceful apartment somewhere far from our house was looking better all the time. To add to the drama, I rained down words of disapproval on a close friend, not realizing the pain they must have inflicted. It seemed I was on an out-of-control roller coaster and couldn't stop. The breaking point always comes, eventually, and mine came with a loud bang.

We've always had an overabundance of computers in our household. Two or three laptops, an office computer and a few older ones stowed away in the closet is not unusual for us. I'm so grateful for these electronic devices, and I am hard pressed to know what I'd do without them. They have been extremely helpful, convenient luxuries for me, especially during all of my writing projects.

When we became a part of the Breakthrough band, in the early years of marriage, it quickly became my job to type and print songs for the group, while also making countless flyers and mailers every year. But getting along with computers in peace and tranquility has definitely not been a part of my job description. I don't know if there's anything in the world more frustrating to me than the supposedly "simple" computer. Trying to understand and keep up with their ever-changing, detailed and complex systems has proven to be utterly maddening. By the time I've finally mastered one program, a newer and better one comes out. I cling to the old and outdated program as long as possible, until it's no longer compatible with anything. Only then will I reluctantly relinquish it, sadly replacing my old program with the new, improved and very complicated version.

My daughters were not much past the toddler years when they were asking for computers of their own. My oldest daughter, Sari's wish for her own laptop came true at the age of seven. It wasn't long until Jessica also proudly held her own computer in her hands. Although the new computers technically belonged to my children, it wasn't unusual for me to use them whenever needed.

Retrieving Jessica's computer from her room one evening after a harried and stressful day, I proceeded to open my previous writings. I was eager to continue the project, happy to finally be doing what I loved. To my great agitation, I couldn't get the word processor to open. Seeing it was locked, I thought it would be easy enough to figure out how to unlock it. An hour later I was still trying. My blood pressure was rising, and I felt the unwanted spirit of anger welling up within me. I knew what was coming. Having spent my whole life trying to overcome the terrible floods of anger, I knew that I needed to shut the computer immediately and walk away from it.

"I'm okay," I told myself. "I'm okay." I had come to understand that God can deliver us from so much, but there are also times in every believer's life when self-control is essential.

I had been taking what felt like giant steps of progress in the area of self-control, so I knew what to do. Getting up, I slammed the computer closed and stepped away. Then something made me stop. I turned, and I glanced back at the hated computer. My fist bunched into a tight little ball. Then I took a step closer to the closed laptop. My clenched fist rose into midair, right above the small computer.

I knew I was putting myself and the computer into a very dangerous position. I hesitated, and contemplated what the outcome would be. I remembered the many times I had given Benji's laptop computer a little punch, and thought it would be harmless enough while also allowing me to vent a little frustration. With one swift, smooth, downward movement, my clenched fist made contact with my daughter's computer. "There, take that!" I muttered, as I walked away.

Halfway across the room, the thought occurred to me to go back and make sure the computer was not damaged. I walked over to the laptop and opened it. The utter despair that coursed through me was indescribable. My heart pounded, and my hands sweated, as I realized what I had done. To my disbelief, the small computer screen had ugly black and grey cracks running all through it. It was ruined. No, it couldn't be ruined! What would Jessica say? My heart was breaking, as I fought back tears. I looked in distress at the broken computer and wondered how I was going to tell her. She was outside at the time, diligently doing her chores.

The horror of it all washed over me in waves, and my shame mingled with the anger that was still lingering. I thought about the horrible week I'd had and felt the full weight of the frustrations that seemed to be mounting with each day. I looked at the computer again, broken and useless.

All of my anger toward that little computer and every other computer in the world rained down on me in that moment. I'd always had a vicious love-hate relationship with those electronic devices; and I remembered all the many times I had longed to beat a computer to smithereens. A very evil thought entered into my mind. I tried to push it away, but it persisted.

No longer resisting its urge, I reached out and took that little computer into my hands and lifted it high above my head.

Holding it for a full three seconds in the air, I again contemplated what the outcome would be. "It's broken anyway," I told myself. "And it deserves this!" The computer hit the tile floor with a terrific crack and flew into pieces. I felt the exhilaration of sweet revenge on all computers ever made. No longer was it controlling me!

I picked up the shattered computer and lifted it high above my head once more. I had reached the point of no return. Down it came again. This time some of its innards came out. In triumph, I picked up its broken shell and slammed it down again! I had always wondered what it might be like to do this very thing, and now I knew. With one last act of indignation, I flung what was left of the computer case into the trash can, satisfied to hear the broken pieces hit the bottom with a resounding thud.

My victory over the computer kingdom was short-lived, however. My daughter's tears smote my soul to the core, and my husband's disappointment in me sent pangs of shame and remorse through my entire being. What was most devastating was the thought of the Almighty God beholding my radical behavior.

I felt I had gone too far this time, and the reality of all the people I'd hurt tormented me. I couldn't forgive myself, and cried bitter tears of remorse. I wondered if I'd ever be happy again. In my mind, I knew God would forgive me as soon as I asked Him, but I couldn't convince my heart of that, and carried a heavy load of terrible shame for several days. I went to bed at night with a heavy heart and woke up in the mornings thinking about how awful I was.

I became ultra-sensitive and very sad, agonizing over my weaknesses. I thought I had left all of this behind me, never again to stoop to this level; but how quickly it had overtaken me again. Because I felt I had so much at stake, it was an extremely painful ordeal. My mind overflowed with negativity, doubts and fears. I saw clearly how my actions had dampened the respect my loving husband had for me and began believing I had tainted our marriage somehow. Moreover, I was fully aware of how my actions had crushed my daughter's tender spirit. What if our children's lives were ruined forever because of my terrible weaknesses?

My husband, who is my knight in shining armor, came to my rescue again. Actually, he sat me down, and spoke very sternly to me. "Kathy," he said, "You are destroying yourself! You will lose everything if you continue on this path of negativity." He lectured me on God's grace and mercy for His children and reminded me of how quickly and surely God will forgive, heal and restore if we ask. My husband urged me to repent, make the needed apologies to people I'd hurt, receive God's forgiveness for it, and get on with life.

I followed my husband's suggestions, and was gradually able to accept total forgiveness, feeling reassured that neither one, Benji or God, was ready to give up on me just yet.

A few days later over breakfast one morning, I opened the Bible, not looking for anything in particular. It fell open to the book of Psalms, and my eyes rested on Psalm 37:23-24. In amazement, I read the words: *"The steps of a good man are ordered by the Lord, and He delights in his way. Though he fall, he shall not be utterly cast down; for the Lord upholds him with His hand."*

Wow! I marveled once again at God's mercy in my life. Though not deserving His grace and comfort, He freely gave it.

Through His divine Word, He let me know in plain terms that His hand was right there, holding me even though I'd fallen. With a grateful heart, I thanked Him, and I knew everything would be okay after all.

> *"Now may the God of peace Himself sanctify you completely; and may your whole spirit, soul, and body be preserved blameless at the coming of our Lord Jesus Christ"* (1Thessalonians 5:23).

Uncontrolled anger is a prevalent problem in today's fast-paced, stressed world. Many Christian men and women are caught in its harmful web, not knowing how to break this painful cycle. Hiding behind a veil of secrecy, the losing battle continues in the Christian and non-Christian world. Many people don't know how to escape these tumultuous rumblings in their hearts.

There are many different reasons for anger problems. In the studies I've done, I found that the emotions resulting from sexual, physical and emotional abuse include shame, rejection, fear, hopelessness and lack of trust. These emotions are all negative feelings that feed the spirit of anger. Many people, not wanting to appear weak or vulnerable, attempt to cover deep pain with anger.

There is also the possibility of anger being passed down spiritually from one generation to the next. If there is a dominant stronghold of anger in several members of one family, that stronghold can continue down through generations. Anger then becomes a generational curse that affects entire families for many years. Whatever the reason, we all know that anger can be very damaging to children, entire families and anyone else who might get in the way. This is why it is important to confront this spirit with boldness, exposing its devious nature before it becomes a major stronghold in our lives. To break the stronghold of anger, we must confront the spirit, confess our weakness and destroy its power through prayer, if we want complete victory.

As I became more familiar with the Bible, I began applying the Scriptures on a much more personal level. Many of the verses I'd previously skimmed over started catching my attention. The words in Ephesians 4:23-24 convicted me: *"Be renewed in the spirit of your mind, and ... put on the new man, which was created according to God, in true righteousness and holiness."*

At the end of the chapter, it states very clearly in verses 29-32 that we, as Christians, should put effort into controlling attitudes such as anger as much as possible: *"Let no corrupt word proceed out of your mouth, but what is good for necessary edification, that it may impart grace to the hearers. And do not grieve the Holy Spirit of God, by whom you were sealed for the day of redemption. Let all bitterness, wrath, anger, clamor and evil speaking be put away from you, with all malice. And be kind to one another, tenderhearted, forgiving one another, even as God in Christ forgave you."*

I had to admit that a lot of these negative emotions were stirring in my own heart. I also knew, if left unchecked, these enemies of the soul would mar the meaningful relationship with God that I desired.

A song I'd sung many times over the years came to my mind. The powerful words from Psalm 51:10-12 stirred my heart:

> *Create in me a clean heart, O God; and renew a right spirit within me.*
>
> *Create in me a clean heart, O God; and renew a right spirit within me.*

Cast me not away from thy presence, O Lord; and take not thy Holy Spirit from me.

Restore unto me the joy of Thy salvation; and renew a right spirit within me.

I knew my emotional healing and balance would come by allowing God's Spirit to tenderize my heart and soul. With His help, I knew I could rid myself completely of the bitterness, wrath and anger that were smoldering within. My eyes opened to see that brokenness and wounds from the past had filled my mind with all kinds of negative and destructive thoughts in the present. I also realized that the process of growing stronger in my spiritual walk simply meant cleaning out those decaying parts of my soul.

My prayer became that of Psalms 139: 23-24: *"Search me O God, and know my heart; try me, and know my anxieties; and see if there is any wicked way in me, and lead me in the way everlasting."* I immediately began to search myself to get rid of all toxic thoughts and feelings in the hidden parts of my heart and mind.

Searching the Bible, I found direction. Promises almost leapt off the pages of the Word. One passage that stuck in my mind and spoke loudly to me was 2 Corinthians 10:3-5: *"For though we walk in the flesh, we do not war according to the flesh. For the weapons of our warfare are not carnal, but mighty in God for* ***pulling down strongholds, casting down arguments, and every high thing that exalts itself against the knowledge of God, bringing every thought into captivity to the obedience of Christ."***

Once again, God's Word brought me back to the simple act of confession. I learned that audibly speaking and confessing my negative thoughts and bringing them into captivity to the Lord pulls down the spiritual strongholds. Yielding to the Holy

Spirit in this way renders evil spirits powerless and allows God to do a work that is supernatural and life-changing. Getting to this level of honesty with myself and with my Creator has been difficult at times. Confessing and exposing the flow of negative thoughts going through my mind hasn't always come easy or felt comfortable, especially when those thoughts have been corrupt or shameful. However, learning to let go of self-consciousness and trusting in God's grace and mercy is the path to wholeness and health for the human spirit.

Another important step to inner healing is the act of forgiveness. Unforgiveness stored up for years and years will always eventually breed anger. Only when we can come to terms with the wrongs done to us and learn to deal with the feelings of resentment because of them, will we be able to find total inner healing. And when the soul is healed, the body is next to be healed. It is only through God that we can be controlled by His Spirit—and be whole in body, mind, soul and spirit.

CHAPTER 17

Forgiveness

"Forgiveness is the scent that the rose leaves on the heel of the one who has crushed it."

-Mark Twain

The mind is complex, containing every detail of our lives. Our carnal, human nature feels that it needs to hold on to every disappointment and heartache, vividly remembering each source of pain. When we live in the flesh instead of living in the Spirit of God, it becomes so easy to dwell on everything hurtful in our past. It's not just the worst of the human race or the deeply wounded and most troubled people who develop pessimistic attitudes about life and are embroiled in spiritual warfare. No, we are all imperfect human beings living in an imperfect world. Bad feelings, twisted emotions and destructive thoughts occur in the life of every person, even those who believe the Gospel.

We can choose to "let it slide," making excuses for our behavior and thoughts. After all, most often, the reasons for our anger, fear and bitterness stem from pain we didn't deserve and certainly didn't request. We can easily develop a victim mentality, pardoning our lack of faith and sinful thoughts with the excuse that we got the "short end of the stick" or simply got a "bad deal" in life. This kind of thinking will leave us feeling victimized and helpless. How many times do we shortchange ourselves by stubbornly clinging to regrets, disappointments and unfortunate things that took place many years ago? Are we allowing the pain of the past to paralyze us, keeping us from enjoying the present and moving into the future? Permitting this kind of negativity to run freely through our minds will open doors to sin and destruction, and will eventually cause us to give up the battle in a spirit of defeat.

Thankfully, we can also choose to empower ourselves, making the decision to stand against the evil in this world. For the past decade, I thought I was doing pretty well in this area. After I was made aware of the power in positive thinking and speaking God's Word over my life's situations, I made every effort to leave the hurtful and unpleasant things of the past far behind me. I stubbornly resolved to pursue a future full of joy. I made the decision to fill my mind with hope, expecting good things to happen to me.

This was a big step forward. My health improved and I definitely felt happier. There are many positive effects of dwelling on the pleasant things in life. The words in Philippians 4:8 say it so well: "*...Whatever things are true, whatever things are noble, whatever things are just, whatever things are pure, whatever things are lovely, whatever things are of good report, if there is any virtue and if there is anything praiseworthy—meditate on these things.*" We are reminded of the benefits of claiming and meditating on God's promises in Proverbs 4:20-22: "*...Give attention to My words; incline your ear to My sayings. Do not let them depart from your eyes; keep them in the midst of your heart; for they are life to those who find them, and health to all their flesh.*"

Life and health sounded good to me, so I put my best efforts forth in staying positive and keeping my focus on good things, until suddenly (at the most inopportune time: during the writing of this book) my emotions suddenly went haywire.

Searching my deepest recollections for accurate details, I was forced to relive some of the anxiety and dread I felt at numerous times. Positive thinking went right out the window and I sank into deep depression for days at a time. Bad feelings, thoughts, and emotions came in floods, overwhelming me. Many were the tears I cried. I had long before gotten accustomed to sadness and tears, so the waves of melancholy that came and went were silently accepted, and seemed to wash and cleanse my soul.

As the months passed by, something else began happening as well. The sadness I felt was slowly giving way to cold feelings coming from somewhere deep inside. This was very troubling to me. I couldn't understand where the brooding, oppressive thoughts were coming from. Over time, I became very bitter, or perhaps a better wording would be "down-right angry." Dark thoughts of resentment inhabited my mind and I was miserable. The angry darts of bitterness were aimed toward the people who had hurt me and the ones who had neglected me; I hashed and rehashed the times of confusion, misunderstanding, rejection, and loneliness. I fumed and sputtered inwardly, silently revolting and lashing out against the mind-control that had been used by others to manipulate my thoughts and decisions.

After several months of feeling particularly cold and unsettled, God began speaking to me. In the trenches of bitterness, my heart was heavy and the pain was sharp. As I cried angry tears into my pillow one night, in a flash, I saw a clear image. This image presented itself repeatedly in my mind and refused to go away. It was a troubling picture of a deep wound that was gruesome, gaping open and lying unprotected.

Throughout the next day, I kept returning to the image, turning it over and over in my mind. I knew God was showing me the state of my own heart. My musings wandered further and I thought about the scars and wounds so many people are afflicted with in life. A story seemed to be shaping, but I couldn't manage to pull it together. Eagerly grasping for more, I begged God to reveal what He was trying to tell me.

Over the next few days, the rest of the story formed in my mind, and I wrote it down as it came to me. Suddenly I realized that this was a revelation from God. I was startled when the realization of what it meant hit me full force.

Below is the illustration God gave me. He showed me why my pain that had been masked for years was suddenly oozing its poisonous venom into my soul again. He also helped me to clearly see the one thing, the only thing in the world that could stop this pain.

It started with a scratch...just one tiny scratch; but against the pale, unblemished surface on the face of my emotions it felt like much more. The suddenness of its unexpected pain was shocking. But as wounds do, especially mere surface wounds, it healed quickly leaving only minimal signs of damage.

Each time it went a little deeper and the pain was sharper. As I watched, I recognized the cruel fingers administering the torture. They were the hands of people I knew: some were the hands of those who didn't really love or care for me, others were the hands of the ones who did care for me but didn't know how to show it, and still others, the hands of those who were simply using me to fulfill selfish desires.

Enduring each wounding in silence, the pain became mysteriously unreal, vague. With each assault the scar healed over tougher, becoming hardened and numb to the touch.

Now, many years later, it has become an open, gaping wound. It's been ripped and torn open many times. No longer given time to heal between assaults, it has become a terrible and fearsome sore: diseased, infected with poison and festering.

Feeling that I won't be able to bear facing the mystery hands that are now inflicting such torment onto my being, I look away. Heart-wrenching pain has gripped me; and I can't remember how it started. I can no longer discern the source of the suffering.

So I blame: I blame it on the unfortunate past that seems a mere haze now. I blame it on life. I blame it on fate that has woven such a web of confusion into my mind, holding me bound against my will. Utter despair overtakes my spirit, and I only want to escape the misery within. The thought comes to mind, to give up the fight—to just accept the wound, no longer resisting the agony it brings, and allow myself to be at the mercy of the assaulting hands.

*But then, something compels me to look again, to look closer. In disbelief, I gasp! What I see, I don't want to acknowledge. It can't be but it is. With remorse and tears I realize, the mystery hands that have been hurting me so badly—the hands that are now continuously reopening my wound, not allowing it to heal—**are my own.***

I fall to my knees. I have one thing on my mind. That one thing is forgiveness. I realize that my pain was real, undeserved and harsh. I know that the hands that should have protected me didn't always do so. And I know that the path I traveled was at times frightening and lonesome.

I also know that as long as I withhold forgiveness and mercy, the pain will prevail. So it is with relief that I eagerly attempt to extend forgiveness, offering its purity and redemption. On the wings of mercy, I soar above the hardness of my own heart and I offer forgiveness and my deep, overflowing love and mercy—all because of the One who did the same for me.

I was ready to forgive. Forgiveness was a subject I had never really given considerable thought. Most of the negative feelings I'd had since childhood were obviously still there, just suppressed. In the hope of finding some kind of relief from my misery, I went through the motions of what I thought was forgiveness, but was disappointed when nothing really changed. I still felt depressed, more than usual, and couldn't shake the anger and bitterness that kept coming to the surface. The following year was a constant struggle.

The breakthrough finally came, when I attended a four-session teaching on forgiveness. Most of what was taught each evening were concepts I'd heard many times over. My mind wandered as the speaker defined forgiveness. It was all information I was familiar with, but as the teachings progressed, I jotted a few things down in my notes, just for good measure:

1. **Forgiveness is cleaning the record of those who have wronged me, and allowing God to love them through me.** Forgive immediately, instantly, quickly.

2. **Forgiveness is allowing God to be responsible for any vengeance or repayment.** "*Beloved, do not avenge yourselves, but rather give place to wrath; for it is written, Vengeance is Mine, I will repay," says the Lord* (Romans 12:19).

3. **Forgiveness is facing the pain directly and choosing to release the offender.** Face the wrongs done to you, calling them for what they are.

This was old material to me. I was slightly disappointed and felt frustrated, wondering if there wasn't anything more to be said on this subject. Then, as if reading my mind, the speaker started talking about what forgiveness is NOT. This was something I definitely had not heard before. This new flow of information grabbed my attention and really got my wheels spinning.

Here's the list of what forgiveness is NOT:

1. **Forgiveness is not a feeling**. Well, yeah I had that one down. There were many times when I went through the motions and forgave people even when I didn't feel like it. I knew that if I'd wait until I felt like doing it, it might never get done.
2. **Forgiveness is not overlooking the wrong done to us**. No problem there. I wasn't one who overlooked anything. I had kept a pretty good record of most wrongs ever done to me.
3. **Forgiveness is not excusing or whitewashing. Sometimes we make excuses or water down the offense, trying to tell ourselves it wasn't as bad as it seemed. This rationalizing is not forgiveness.** This is when the lights started coming on. Yes, this was me. I was stunned, definitely guilty.
4. **Forgiveness is not using psychology to understand the offender. Understanding what happened is important. Understanding why the person acted as they did is important. But understanding and forgiving are two different things.** Now the "breakthrough" was happening. I'm a mercy-motivated person, so my natural response to people who offend or hurt me is to first find some excuse for their behavior, and then find out why it happened. When I feel like I understand them and their twisted reasons for the offense, I automatically feel like I've forgiven them. The truth is that the real focus of forgiveness should not be placed on

WHY it happened, but on the fact that it DID happen, and WAS wrong, and now that I've acknowledged that I CAN CHOOSE to forgive and release the offender.

5. **Forgiveness is not taking blame for the wrong. Assuming the blame for what was done against us may feel righteous, but it is not forgiveness.** Bingo again! I rarely took the entire blame for offenses, but in almost every bad situation, I would tend to take some of the blame.

Now I had something to work with. The detailed definition and explanation of forgiveness helped me see this essential concept in a different light. When I stopped excusing the offender, stopped rationalizing the wrong he/she had done, and stopped taking the blame for other people's actions, I had nothing left but the offense and how it made me feel. I had nothing but my pain and the grim reality of the situation. Finally, I could call it what it was and process the hurt properly, allowing myself to feel the full force of it. Then I could choose to forgive, releasing the offender to the throne of God, acknowledging that what he/she had done was wrong, but making the choice to forgive the wrong done.

I had previously thought that covering my anger or bitterness was somehow righteous and holy, but in all reality there was nothing holy about it. By denying my true feelings, I was just allowing the bitterness to remain inside of me, festering and growing more with each passing day. By covering the pain, I was simply living in denial and making the situation worse.

"If we could read the secret history of our enemies, we would find in each person's life sorrow and suffering enough to disarm all hostility." –Henry Wadsworth Longfellow

True forgiveness is so important, not only because it releases God's power to work in our own lives, but it also releases God's power to work in the life of the offender. Even in His darkest hour, when Jesus hung and died on the cross for a crime He didn't commit, He cried out to His Father God saying, *"Father, forgive them, for they do not know what they do."* Isaiah 53:5 reminds us of the heavy price He freely paid for the forgiveness of our sins. *"But He was wounded for our transgressions, He was bruised for our iniquities; the chastisement of our peace was upon Him, and by His stripes we are healed."* Because of His death and resurrection, we are automatically forgiven for every sin we've committed, when we accept Him as our personal Savior and ask for His forgiveness.

Therefore, we are also able to forgive the people who offend us, no matter how difficult it may seem, through the power of the Holy Spirit. Once we get the whole picture and understand it clearly, we will see that withholding forgiveness is not a wise option for anyone. When we refrain from forgiving others, so does God for us. That is the scary part of unforgiveness, something we often do not take seriously enough. Matthew 6: 14-15 foretells the end result of transgressing in this area: *"For if you forgive men their trespasses, your heavenly Father will also forgive you. But if you do not forgive men their trespasses, neither will your Father forgive your trespasses."*

Refusing to forgive others also has the power to prevent prayers from being answered and miracles from manifesting in our lives. As far as our physical bodies go, unforgiveness wreaks havoc on good health and peace of mind. To find true stability and peace in life, we need forgiveness. Otherwise, we will be bound up in a prison we've made for ourselves. *"Unforgiveness is the ultimate self-victimization. There is no prison so strong, nor so foolish, as the one of our own making."* —(Anonymous)

On the very last evening of the teachings on forgiveness, we were given a written prayer with appropriate spaces to fill in names of the people we wanted to forgive. I went through this prayer many times, each time forgiving those who I felt had wronged me, one by one. Now that I knew what true forgiveness should be, it came easy to allow myself to feel the pain, and to release my hurts and past resentments, leaving them at the feet of Jesus. It felt really good. I felt light and free as I crossed more and more people off the formidable list of the "unforgiven."

When forgiving people, I like having a specific prayer to read, because it allows me to simply think about my feelings rather than groping for the right words to say. Because it has helped me so much to use the following prayer written by Steve Stutzman, I want to share it with each person who reads this book, and give you the opportunity to use it in the same way I have. Simply say the prayer out loud, filling in the spaces with as much honesty as you can muster up:

Our Father in heaven, I come before you today in Jesus' name. Father God, I have been hurt, tremendously wounded. Only You truly understand this pain.

Lord, You remember the day when ______________________________

____

____.

I am coming to You today with this wound, the pain, the lies I have believed because of it, and my sin of unforgiveness.

Right now, I bring ______________________(name) to Your throne, God. According to Your Word, I choose to forgive him/her. I release him/her before Your throne, and as long as I live, he/she owes me nothing.

Father, when this happened I felt very ______________________

____.

I began to believe ______________________________________
____.

Also, I was angry at _______________________________ for hurting me, and I got bitter at him/her.

Today I bring this as sin, and I lay it at the foot of the cross. I repent of believing lies about myself and You. I repent of my unforgiveness and bitterness through the blood of Jesus Christ, and I renounce the spirit of bitterness. I command that spirit to leave me in Jesus' name. I ask You, heavenly Father to reclaim for Yourself the ground I had surrendered to evil by this sin.

Father, as I release this offense and my sin today, I also bring my pain. You said, Lord, that Jesus Christ, my Savior, was chastised for my peace and I am healed by His stripes.

I desperately need healing—so today I bring this pain I have lived in, and I lay it into the lash-marks on Jesus Christ. Please heal me, Father.

Thank You, heavenly Father. Thank you, Lord Jesus Christ, for carrying MY sin and MY pain to Calvary.

Wash me thoroughly from my iniquity, and cleanse me from my sin. In Jesus' precious name. Amen!

I discovered that I was also holding a shockingly large amount of unforgiveness and hatred toward myself, which was wreaking havoc in my personal life and emotions. I realized that it was just as important to forgive myself as others, maybe even more important.

Unforgiveness toward self will always eventually breed self-hatred. Self-hatred is extremely volatile, a wicked and destructive spirit that corrodes the soul and destroys a person's self-image. Self-hatred is never an act of humility, but rather a slap in the face of our Creator. We are made in the image of God by God; we are His creation. We should be able to appreciate who we are just for that reason alone, if for none other.

Furthermore, who do we spend more time with than ourselves? Of course, the answer is, "No one." We can get away from others who annoy us, but we can never escape "self," not for one second. I mean, seriously, we can't even go to the bathroom without ourselves! So we may as well face the things we don't like about ourselves, make peace with them and get on with life and loving ourselves for who we are.

In the past, I have regularly let my mind wander, and have dwelled on the negative things in life entirely too much. This led to having a negative and distorted view of myself. Instead of seeing the person I was actually created to be, I could only see my carnality and failures. The judgments and opinions of other people chimed in with my own accusing voice, leaving me with a heavy burden of discouragement.

How much better this world would be if we could shut out the other voices, and simply wrap our hearts and minds around the things God says about us! People's opinions are just that—opinions. But God is our Creator, and He knows our capabilities and the tremendous potential we have through Him. His power goes to work in our lives the second we take our eyes off the things that are wrong with us, and start dwelling on what God's Word has to say about us. Everyone's true identity and value can only be found in Jesus Christ. The things He has to say about us are the things that really matter in life. Here is a list of some of the best confessions of faith you can make:

I am a child of God . . . . Ephesians 1:5, Romans 8:16

I am born again. . . . . 1 Peter 1:23

I am in Christ. . . . . 1 Corinthians 1:30

Christ is in me .... John 14:20

God's Spirit is within me .... Ezekiel 36:27

I am a new creature .... 2 Corinthians 5:17

I am saved by grace........................ Ephesians 2:8

I am His workmanship..................... Ephesians 2:10

I am forgiven .... Colossians 1:13-14

I am clean....................................... John 15:3

I am washed....................... 1 Corinthians 6:11

I am holy and without blame .... Ephesians 1:4

I am free .... Galatians 5:1

I am the righteousness of God............. 2 Corinthians 5:21

I am sanctified..................... 1 Corinthians 6:11

I am justified .... Romans 5:1

My inward man is being renewed day by day 2 Corinthians 4:16

I am being transformed by the renewing of my mind Romans 12:2

I am walking in newness of life .... Romans 6:4

I am the Lord's sheep and He is my Shepherd....... Psalms 23:1

I am my Beloved's and He is mine .... Song of Solomon 6:3

I am casting all my cares on Jesus .... 1 Peter 5:7

I am strengthened with might through His Spirit Ephesians 3:16

I can do all things through Christ............ Philippians 4:13

I am being prospered; I have hope and a future.. Jeremiah 29:11

I am an heir of God and a joint-heir with Jesus.... Romans 8:17

I am chosen by God.............................. John 15:16

I am called out of darkness into His light .... 1 Peter 2:9

I am preserved from all evil by God............ Psalms 121:7-8

I am protected from the enemy.................. Isaiah 59:19

I am delivered from powers of darkness .... Colossians 1:13

I am protected by angels .... Psalms 91:11

I am walking by faith, not by sight .... 2 Corinthians 5:7

I am taught by the Holy Spirit..................... John 14:26

I am guided into all truth .... John 16:13

I am crucified with Christ .... Galatians 2:20

I am buried with Christ...................... Colossians 2:12

I am risen with Christ .... Colossians 2:12-13

I am seated with Christ in heavenly places...... Ephesians 2:6

I am the head and not the tail .... Deuteronomy 28:13

I am above only and not beneath.......... Deuteronomy 28:13

I am in the body of Christ .... 1 Corinthians 12: 12-13

I am surrounded by the righteous............... Psalms 142:7

I am blessed .... Acts 3:26

My desires are being fulfilled.............. Psalms 145:18-19

Goodness and mercy follow me all my days .... Psalms 23:6

I am healed by His stripes .... 1 Peter 2:24

I am complete in Christ .... Colossians 2:9-10

I am an overcomer .... 1 John 4:4

I am more than a conqueror through Christ....... Romans 8:37

I am a branch of the true vine.................. John 15:1-5

I am rooted and built up in Him .... Colossians 2:6-7

I am established in the faith .... Colossians 2:6-7

I am the temple of the Holy Spirit........... 1 Corinthians 6:19

I am a partaker of His divine nature .... 2 Peter 1:4

I am the salt of the earth .... Matthew 5:13

I am the light of the world .... Matthew 5:14

I am an ambassador for Christ. . . . . 2 Corinthians 5:20
I am loved by Jesus . . . . John 15:9
I am loved by the Father. . . . . John 16:27
I am filled with the love of God. John 17:26
I am free from condemnation . . . . Romans 8:1
I have been redeemed from destruction. . . . . Psalms 103:2-5
I have been turned away from my iniquities . . . . Acts 3:26
I have been cleansed from all unrighteousness. . . . . 1 John 1:9
I have been abundantly pardoned . . . . Isaiah 55:7
I have been reconciled to God. . . . . 2 Corinthians 5:18
I have been given power, love and a sound mind . . 2 Timothy 1:7
I have put my trust in God . . . . Psalms 56:3-4
I have a new heart and a new spirit. . . . . Ezekiel 36:26
I have the mind of Christ. . . . . 1 Corinthians 2:16
I have the joy of Jesus . . . . John 17:13
I have redemption through His blood . . . . Colossians 1:14
I have power over the enemy. . . . . Luke 10:19
I have victory. . . . . 1 Corinthians 15:57
I have grace and peace. . . . . 2 Peter 1:2, John 14:27
I have sufficiency in all things. . . . . 2 Corinthians 9:8
I have abundant life . . . . John 10:10
I have eternal life. . . . . John 3:16

We need to constantly remind ourselves that we can never give up the fight. No matter how discouraged we may be or how defeated and diminished we feel, we must always take one more step in the right direction. We must keep fighting the battle for peace with ourselves, with the people in our lives and with our Creator.

I know I speak for all people when I say this: I don't want to come to the end of my journey on earth just to realize that life could have been richer, healthier and far more enjoyable than it was. I don't want to miss out on the life that has been promised to us, simply because I failed to tap into God's redeeming, life-changing, and healing power of forgiveness—the gift of peace with others and self.

The Lord's Prayer

(Matthew 6:9-13)

"Our Father in heaven, hallowed be Your name.

Your kingdom come. Your will be done
on earth as it is in heaven.

Give us this day our daily bread.

And forgive us our debts, as we forgive our debtors.

And do not lead us into temptation,
but deliver us from the evil one.

For Yours is the kingdom and the power
and the glory forever. Amen."

SECTION FIVE

Becoming A True Believer

Show me Your ways, O Lord;
teach me Your paths. Lead me in Your truth,
and teach me, for You are the God of my
salvation; on You I wait all day. (Psalms 25: 4-5)

CHAPTER 18

Keeping it Simple

The further along I travel on this journey through life, the more I come to see that being a true believer is not complex, but is actually much simpler than we've made it. Unfortunately, for the most part, the path that led me to God was a long, winding, twisting and turning trail of confusion. In the hope of preventing others from experiencing the frustrations I've encountered, I want to share the key things that have opened many doors to God's blessings for me, and have made the last decade of my Christian walk enjoyable and rewarding. There were four definite milestones that have been real and meaningful to me and have made a significant difference in my life:

1. **By faith receive the gift of salvation through Jesus' blood on the cross.**
2. **Repent and turn away from sin.**
3. **Build an intimate relationship with Jesus.**
4. **Love all people.**

I will share the value of each of these milestones with you, how each one touched my life in a very personal way, and how these milestones can change your life as well. I believe these steps of faith are important and required in the life of every true believer.

1. **By faith receive the gift of salvation through Jesus' blood on the cross.**

This is the first step of faith. Many people cannot grasp believing in a God they cannot see in person, so they resist Him and His call on their lives. To the ones who question the Christian faith, I simply say, "Try it for yourself and see if it's real." God challenges us to discover Him: *"You will seek Me and find Me, when you search for Me with all your heart. I will be found by you, says the Lord"* (Jeremiah 29:13-14a).

That is why it is so important to exercise faith. Having faith is the act of believing without seeing. Hebrews 11:1 tells us that *"Faith is the substance of things hoped for, the evidence of things not seen,"* and verse 6 reminds us that *"...without faith it is impossible to please God."* Then comes the question, "How can I build my faith?"

Romans 10:17 tells us that *"Faith comes by hearing, and hearing by the Word of God."* Earlier in that same chapter, verses 8-9, say, *"The Word is near you, in your mouth and in your heart...that if you confess with your mouth the Lord Jesus and believe in your heart that God has raised Him from the dead, you will be saved. For with the heart one believes unto righteousness, and with the mouth confession is made unto salvation."* Becoming familiar with the Bible, keeping the Word in your mouth and in your heart, and confessing the Word will convince you of its truth, and keep you grounded in faith.

Being a child of God and living for Him is a rewarding way of life, far exceeding the aimless wanderings of a life that is alone and unprotected. I am not implying that trials, disappointments and hard times will never come our way again. We're not promised a life free of hardships or pain. However, Jesus tells us in Matthew 11:28-30: *"Come to Me, all you who labor and are heavy laden, and I will give you rest. Take My yoke upon you and learn from Me, for I am gentle and lowly in heart, and you will find rest for your souls. For My yoke is easy and My burden is light."*

Being able to lean on a God whose strength is unlimited eases the difficult times. He says in 2 Corinthians 12:9: *"My grace is sufficient for you, for My strength is made perfect in weakness."* I've found these verses to be true. It's amazing how things start taking a turn for the better when I admit my weakness and ask for God's help. He rewards humility and shows mercy to those who cry out to Him. Even in the midst of hard times, those who are connected to God and depend on Him will be rewarded with peace of mind and clear direction. The promise in Hebrews 11:16b is certainly true, where we are reminded: *"He is a rewarder of those who diligently seek Him."*

I've never seen God physically or had visions in which He appeared to me. I've never heard His audible voice, though many have. But I've seen His power in more ways than I could mention. I've felt His Presence, and experienced His grace, mercy, forgiveness and compassion. I've been delivered from sins that held me bound for years, through the power of His Word and through the relationship I have with Him. He has given me confidence and restored and made whole the broken and wounded spirit I once had. He satisfies my desires, bringing the most exciting things to completion in my life, often in the most unexpected ways.

So it is not difficult for me to believe without seeing. It is not difficult to serve this great and mighty God, who rewards me daily with His peace and gives me joy in living. Yes, I know by personal experience that He is also a rewarder of those who diligently *serve* Him.

The first step to serving God is the simple act of surrendering your life to Him. As you make the decision to submit to Him, remember that God created you, understands you and knows all about you. He has been waiting for this moment ever since you were born, and He will come to you, quickly and surely. He formed and created you. You are amazing to Him. Even though you feel flawed and your life may be in tatters, He loves you with a love like no other.

Very simply, in your own words, whether eloquent and detailed, or halting and simple, just ask Jesus Christ to come into your heart and become the Redeemer and Lord of your life. Give your heart and the remainder of your life to Him, and ask Him to cover you with His protection. Ask Him to strengthen you and restore you from your broken condition. Come to Him just as you are, and give yourself and all you are to Him. He will hear your words, and you will immediately become His child. Then you will begin a new journey into an exciting future with Him.

Become a true believer, a child of God, saved from eternal destruction by your faith in Him and His grace for you. Seek Him with all your heart, and trust Him to make Himself known to you.

2. Repent and turn away from sin.

Some people assume that turning away from sin comes naturally and easily after people accept Christ as their personal Savior, but I'm not so sure. I've always had a reverence for God and wanted His presence in my life. I've had a relationship with Him from early childhood. But even so, my conscience became dull, and my heart, hardened. I disregarded His authority for years, in many ways.

This lapse in faith can happen very quickly in the lives of believers. Life is a mysterious thing and takes many unexpected twists and turns. Because of hardships, mistreatment and disappointments, many people lose their ability to feel anymore, becoming cold to those around them and numbing themselves to the pain. How well I can relate to that story! This is a very dangerous place to be. By allowing ourselves to become numb to the pain, we can also, without realizing it, be numbing our spirits, no longer being sensitive to what's right and wrong.

I lived under this 'anesthesia' for many years. Not knowing what to do with the physical and emotional pain I carried in my heart, I shut down my emotions in many areas. I did not realize that by doing this, I was also numbing my conscience. This gave place to sin in my life.

My conscience convicted me many times and kept me from entering into the deepest realms of darkness. I'm thankful for the part of my conscience that would not be silent. I feel that it protected me many times. But there were parts of me that my conscience couldn't reach. I became spiritually insensitive to several deep-rooted sins in my life. I felt no conviction in those areas, even though I knew my actions were wrong and displeasing to God. Over time, the deceptions in my mind became strongholds of tremendous power.

A stronghold can either have a positive or negative effect on your life. When you build your life and beliefs on Jesus Christ, He will become your Stronghold, and that of course is GOOD. Most of the time, however, when we refer to a stronghold, we mean a deep-rooted sin that has taken a firm hold on us and won't allow us to live in complete victory. Many otherwise good people allow strongholds to take root, and because of deception and a dull conscience, become immune to the problem areas in their lives.

That is exactly where I found myself, caught in a web of deception, denying the depth of my sin and the damage it was doing. Even though I knew there were issues in my life that were unresolved, and there were temptations lingering all around to which I occasionally yielded, I thought I was doing a pretty good job of being a Christian. Silencing the guilt that came with disobedience, I comforted myself with the fact that I had given my heart to the Lord, and made a verbal commitment to Him. I didn't realize the importance of confirming my commitment to Jesus Christ with a life that was fully committed to honoring Him with obedience and right choices.

I believe this is one of the biggest deceptions in the world today. People like to believe they are saved by a special grace that will grant them God's favor, even though they're living a life of compromise, mediocrity and disrespect to their Maker. But there is really nothing noble in that. No meaningful and worthwhile relationship requires only the words, "I believe in you," and "I am yours forever," while the person saying them goes on to prove otherwise by disrespectful actions and deeds. Very few people continue blessing, accepting and loving friends who are defying, disregarding, trampling on their mercy, coming to them only when they have a need. Don't we all desire pure relationships that include accountability, respect and love? We do not want a surface love, but love that is deep enough to bring submission. We all know that when those elements are missing, the relationship will crumble. Then there will be rejection and separation.

With that thought in mind, can we really expect God to continue blessing us and pouring out His best on us if we don't show Him honor and respect, and walk in submission to Him? Can we really ask that of the God of the universe, when we as lowly humans would never tolerate that in our own earthly relationships? A belief system that doesn't require honoring and reverencing the God who formed and created us is worthless. The words, "God, I believe in you and accept you into my heart," are truly empty unless followed by a life of obedience. James 2:19-20 touches on this subject: *"You believe that there is one God. You do well. Even the demons believe—and tremble! But do you want to know, O foolish man, that faith without works is dead?"*

Jesus tells us in John 14:15: *"If you love Me, keep My commandments."* We can also read the sobering words in Exodus 20:4b: *"For I, the Lord your God, am a jealous God, visiting the iniquity of the fathers upon the children to the third and fourth generations of those who hate Me."* By continuing to give in to temptations, according to God's Word, we could be in danger of placing the curse of our sins on our children and grandchildren, to the third and fourth generations. We owe it to God, to ourselves and to our children to live upright lives, as much as we possibly can in our mortal condition. In Proverbs 3:33b we read, *"He blesses the home of the just."* I believe our marriages, families and our children's lives will be improved dramatically just by us putting forth our best our efforts to please God.

He is a God of mercy for those who call on Him. Exodus 20 goes on to say in verse 6: *"But showing mercy to thousands, to those who love Me and keep My commandments."* Those who are desperate to overcome temptations and serve Him will never be turned away. The Bible says He will come quickly to them and will have mercy on them, and will deliver them from all their sorrows. Psalm 34:18 pledges: *"The Lord is near to those who have a broken heart; and saves such as have a contrite spirit."* In Psalm 91:14 the Lord also speaks fondly of those who love Him, know Him, and call on Him: *"Because he has set his love upon Me, therefore I will deliver him. I will set him on high, because he has known My name. He shall call upon Me, and I will answer him; I will be with him in trouble; I will deliver him and honor him."*

My husband helped me see the destruction that was raining down on my life and emotions because of unconfessed sin in my past and present life. He helped me to face and remove the strongholds that held me prisoner, confessing and turning away from them. By surrendering and relinquishing those things to God, I was truly making Jesus the Lord of my life, and believing that His power could break the hold of the enemy. As my slate was wiped clean, I felt a load of weight lift from my shoulders.

You can feel the load of sin and sorrow lift from your life too. God will quickly pardon you from your sins as you confess them to Him, asking for His forgiveness. There is nothing He doesn't already know about you, so you can be completely honest, even baring your deepest thoughts. The power of confession is mighty and will crush any satanic hold on you, releasing you to walk in freedom: *"If we confess our sins, He is faithful and just to forgive us our sins and to CLEANSE us from all unrighteousness* (1 John 1:9). *"He who covers his sins will not prosper, but whoever CONFESSES AND FORSAKES THEM will have mercy"* (Proverbs 28:13).

The life that brings satisfaction, fulfillment, strength and true happiness is the life that is lived in submission to God and His kingdom. Striving to please God and offering Him a life of excellence will not only enhance your relationship with Him, but will also bring pleasures and rewards to your life that you could have never dreamed.

Some people say that it's impossible to overcome the temptations, addictions and strongholds in their lives, but God says in Romans 8:37, *"In all these things we are more than conquerors through Him who loved us."* Ephesians 3:20reminds us that He *"is able to do exceedingly, abundantly above all that we ask or think, according to the power that works in us."*

Don't be deceived by believing that you can attempt to nourish your soul with the corrupted 'food' this world offers (the lust of the eye, the lust of the flesh and the pride of life), while claiming to be a child of God. This will only bring confusion and defeat to your life. James 1:8 (KJV) warns us that *"A double minded man* [or woman] *is unstable in all his* [or her] *ways."* Those who choose to dishonor God with a compromised lifestyle, while claiming to be redeemed by a special grace that covers and hides sin, are living a double life. This kind of existence is unstable and weak. Such individuals rarely enjoy long-term success or peace of mind. They usually end up broken and defeated emotionally, financially and physically. This I know from experience.

Proverbs 16:3 encourages you to: *"Commit your works to the Lord, and your thoughts will be established."* The NIV gives this passage a unique slant: *"Commit to the Lord whatever you do, and your plans will succeed."* According to these scriptures, true repentance and turning away from sin will do more than simply release you from the powers of darkness. It will also open the door to God's blessings, and you will enjoy seeing His power released and His plans fulfilled through your life.

3. Build an intimate relationship with Jesus.

When it comes to our relationship with Jesus, we cannot be too open and honest. He wants to have an intimate, deep relationship with every person. We were created to follow after Him and worship Him, sharing every area of our lives, thoughts and emotions with Him. There is nothing quite as exciting as having an intimate relationship with the Creator of the universe. Having a close walk with the One who created us will make life richer, easier and much more pleasant.

Even the most outgoing 'people persons' have periods of loneliness in this world, times when they find themselves completely alone. When there's no one to talk to, or you're in a situation that doesn't allow you to speak freely with other people, God is the One who will always be there. He will send His Spirit to comfort you and give direction in any situation you encounter.

Knowing there's always Someone who will never leave you, and who loves and cares about you is a wonderful thing.

Another reason close intimacy with God is rewarding is because it brings a spirit of peace. When you're happy, offering thankfulness and praise in worship brings a warm sense of gratefulness and peace. When you're upset or worried, you'll feel less anxious when you unload your troubles to the Lord, because He will immediately begin to lift the burden from your shoulders, easing your mind. Peace of mind is persistently sought by every human being, and is best fulfilled through having a close connection and intimacy with God.

Of course, every person will have moments of temptation. There's no escaping that reality of life. There are times I struggle terribly with wrong desires that try to pull me in and get their grip on me. In the heat of those moments, I have only found one way to avoid getting caught in their clutches and carried away completely, and that is, through being open and honest about the situation with God.

Sometimes in the past I wanted to conceal things in my mind, and thought I could avoid talking to God about certain subjects, thinking maybe He wouldn't notice if I didn't point it out. Of course, in my heart of hearts, I knew that was ridiculous. Still, I found myself often holding things in, not being able to release everything to God. Luke 8:17 explains just how futile it is to hide from God: *"For nothing is secret that will not be revealed; nor anything hidden, that will not be known and come to light."* Since He knows everything anyway, we may as well make up our minds to stay intimately connected to God, sharing everything in our lives with Him.

At one time, I thought that if things would only start going better in my life and I could get closer to perfection, then I would finally have a deeper, more intimate and meaningful relationship with God. Now I realize that I had it all backwards. The meaningful, intimate relationship with Him actually needed to come first, and I needed to stop trying so hard on my own. The key to a happy and satisfying life is not in striving so hard for perfection, but rather in being able to recognize and confess our imperfections. All we really need to do is become vulnerable, telling Him our weaknesses and fears, and Jesus Christ will make His strength known. His overflowing concern toward us is revealed in the promise of 2 Corinthians 12:9b: *"My strength is made perfect in weakness."* When *He* strengthens us, it is supernatural. God's power is strong enough to overcome evil and break strongholds. His power is real, and changes lives.

While going through a very difficult time many years ago, I experienced deliverance that can only come by being completely open and transparent with God. I was struggling more than ever before. I've often wondered (sarcastically) if there was a sign on my back that said, "Target for temptation, right over here." Unfortunately, we are all in a world where temptations will be all around us every day. Every person has specific weaknesses that can hinder his or her walk with God. No one is above the curse of wrong desires and sin. The only thing that can break that curse is the power of Jesus Christ working in and through our lives.

This particular temptation was great. I had made the firm choice to resist its pull, so I felt sure that I wouldn't buckle and give in to its power again; but I was using all of my energy trying to fight the battle, and I was miserable. The desire was still there so strong, and the misery I felt was crushing my spirit. The temptation brought unrest and turmoil to my mind, never giving me a minute of peace.

Since I have a deep need to talk when things are bothering me, I finally spoke to someone I trusted, seeking some kind of relief, only to be deeply hurt by her response. I had already said all I could say to my husband, so I was now left with no one on the earth to share my troubles.

One evening, when wrestling with the turmoil in my mind, the thought came to me that God knew all about me already. He knew every thought, heard every sigh, and saw every tear. I realized how very safe I was with Him. He would listen patiently while I spoke, even if it continued for hours. He surely wouldn't reject me, and wouldn't tell anyone else what I told Him. He alone held the power in His hands to help me.

With a hopeful heart, I entered into the quietness of my bedroom, not bothering to turn on the lights. The darkness in the room seemed to match the state of my soul. Sinking down onto the bed, I sat hunched over, hands hanging in my lap, feet sprawled out in front of me. There was silence as I took a few minutes to gather my scattered thoughts.

Then I spoke hesitantly into the darkness. I spoke to Him as if He were there in person and invited His presence to come into the room. Quite simply, I said, "God, I ask you to come, because I have something I need to talk to you about." I felt a tinge of hope, and my self-consciousness gave way to desperation. I spoke aloud into the room, earnestly, confessing in detail the depth of my sin and the state of my soul. For several hours I stayed in the darkness of the room, communicating with my Maker on a deeper and more intimate level than ever before.

As I spoke, I could feel the satanic hold on me loosening. That evening, I experienced the mighty deliverance of my Savior, Jesus Christ. Because of the simple act of honest confession, I was unexpectedly and supernaturally changed. Over the course of the next several days I discovered that I no longer had to deal with those unwanted thoughts and desires because they were gone. I experienced what He promised in 1John 1:9: *"If we confess our sins, He is faithful and just to forgive us our sins and to cleanse us from all unrighteousness."*

There's so much in the Bible about the power of confession. I can identify with the verses in Psalm 32:5-6a: *"I acknowledged my sin to You, and my iniquity I have not hidden. I said, I will confess my transgressions to the Lord, and You forgave the iniquity of my sin... For this cause everyone who is godly shall pray to You in a time when You may be found."* Verse seven in that same chapter confirms what I've already experienced to be true: *"You are my hiding place; You shall preserve me from trouble; You shall surround me with songs of deliverance."*

When I discovered the tremendous power in intimacy and open communication with God, my trust in His power became stronger. Instead of wrestling with temptation on my own strength—which isn't usually very affective anyway—I know it will dissolve much more quickly if I do nothing but simply confess it to God, exposing my heart and hiding nothing.

Through confession, I bring into the light every evil scheme and tactic that's been so slyly presented to me, thereby rendering the works of darkness powerless. The enemy wants to stay hidden in the recesses of the heart and in the darkness surrounding sin, because these are the only places demonic powers can work. Jesus is the light of the world, and where there is light, there can be no darkness. We need to stay connected and close to Him, because He is our protector and shelter, our strong tower and our shield.

4. Love all people.

"You shall love the Lord your God with all your heart, with all your soul and with all your mind. This is the first and greatest commandment. And the second is like it: you shall love your neighbor as yourself" (Matthew 22:37-39). These are strong words and a direct commandment from Jesus. Of all God's

commands, I believe this may be one of the most overlooked, and the most difficult to fulfill. How many times do we hear ourselves murmuring bitterly about the people in our lives? Some of us have even been guilty of making the statement, "My life would be much better if it weren't for the people in it!"

I've always been a person who enjoys being in public. I like meeting new folks and have developed many rewarding friendships over the years. However, I'm not satisfied with shallow relationships. In fact, I thrive in close, sincere friendships with open communication and honesty. I prefer to have just a few really good friends rather than a ton of casual friends. I will quickly become open, vulnerable and painfully honest with the people I trust. Therefore, I choose my good friends carefully, because these friendships lead to valuable, treasured relationships.

It's so easy to love those we connect with on a deeper level. Being with close friends brings happiness and fulfillment to our lives. We interact with them differently. We are naturally loving and caring with our closest friends. We show our finest side. It's easy to see that we have the love of God surging and flowing through us when we are with them. This kind of love is a beautiful thing.

But then there are always those 'special' people in our lives too. You know the ones I'm talking about; we all have them. These are the 'friends' who drive us crazy. We wonder how God could have ever allowed them to cross our path. Worse yet, we have no idea how these troublesome people became permanent fixtures in our lives. For instance, even if we can't stand our in-laws, we know that we must be friends with them because they're family. Then there may be the next-door neighbor who is annoying, rude and spiteful. Are we supposed to love that person too? What about a hateful boss who doesn't appreciate your best efforts? Don't forget about your so-called best friend, who does anything but make your life better. The list could go on and on. We ask ourselves, "Why is it so important for me to love these people?" and we often follow up with the inevitable question, "How can they be so unlovable?"

In a world of countless misunderstandings, rudeness, thoughtlessness, backbiting and slander, what does God tell us to do? He tells us to love other people as much as we love ourselves, plain and simple. There are no loopholes or ways to get around it, nor are there ways to sugarcoat our actions. We cannot pretend with outward graciousness, while hiding malicious thoughts inside. God can clearly see the deceitfulness of our hearts as well as He can see our outward dealings with people.

Then we wonder why it's so important to God that we love every individual who comes into our lives. Can't we tell a few irritating people off in the world, letting them know how absolutely infuriating their behavior really is? Is it always right to turn the other cheek, allowing people to hurt us more, allowing them to stomp us further into the ground? Shouldn't we stand up and defend ourselves?

I have a deep need for justice. When I see others being mistreated, I am quick to come to their aid, defending them whenever I can. I also strongly dislike manipulation, deception or emotional abuse of any kind. I do not respect anyone who engages in these hurtful behaviors. Neither do I have a problem defending myself and rarely shrink back in the face of unfairness or bullying.

I experienced the power of self-defense at a young age. Believing I had no one to protect me, I fought back and violently attacked my abuser. This literally set me free. My feelings of hopelessness were quickly replaced with victory, freedom and most importantly, safety. With these heartaches tucked away in my memory, I developed a tough-girl mentality and took great pride in that attitude for many years. As many people tend to do, I took my attitude too far. I equipped myself with all the smart answers, retorts and every form of revenge imaginable. I determined silently to never again be hurt or victimized. No, never again! With each year that passed, it seemed my heart became more hardened, and my spirit became tougher. I carefully guarded myself, and did not hesitate to stand up to people who challenged me, even if it meant hurting or degrading them in some way.

After I rededicated my life to God and started digging deeper into the Bible, I experienced more and more discomfort when reading the words in Matthew 5:38-39: *"You have heard that it was said, 'An eye for an eye, and a tooth for a tooth.'"* I thought, "Yeah, preach it!" Unfortunately for me, it goes on to say, *"But I tell you not to resist an evil person. But whoever slaps you on your right cheek, turn the other to him also."*

To make matters worse, my husband wasn't impressed with my cantankerous ways. Benji's most common, and most irritating, phrase became, "Just let it go, Kathy." To my further irritation, he constantly reminded me of the famous verse I just quoted. Furthermore, he would often ask me in that questioning tone, "Do you call what you did 'turning the other cheek'?"

I was quick to answer with an equally spiritual retort, "But I'm a child of the God most High, and no one has the right to treat me badly!"

Unfortunately, bringing God into our battles and spiritualizing them does not make them right. The Lord very clearly says that we need to walk in love and not to fight back when someone merely treats us unfairly. Does this mean that we should be like limp rag dolls that others can trample underfoot? No, of course it doesn't. We are all very valuable in the eyes of God, and it is never right for one person to abuse another. Victims of any kind of abuse need to tell someone they trust. They need to get help immediately. Abuse is prevalent in our world today, and we should never tolerate it in any form.

However, we all know that there are many other less direct, but very hurtful ways we attack each other. Some of the most common forms of hurting other people include gossip, slander, degradation and contempt. These actions are in direct competition with love. They feed anger, hatred and bad feelings. It seems that human nature delights in bringing others down; and somehow, we find ourselves believing that tearing others down will lift us up in some way. This kind of thinking is self-serving and untrue.

True power, true victory and the greatest blessings of life can only come through God—and God is all about love. Such divine love isn't just the soft, comfortable kind of love we all extend to those who are kind to us and treat us fairly. No, it also includes loving those who don't love us and those who are making life difficult for us. Christ plainly instructs us in Matthew 5:44-45: *"But I say to you, love your enemies, bless those who curse you, do good to those who hate you, and pray for those who spitefully use you and persecute you, that you may be the sons of your Father in heaven; for He makes His sun rise on the evil and on the good, and sends rain on the just and on the unjust."* Earlier in the same chapter, in verses 11-12a, Jesus reveals God's compensation to true believers who are unfairly treated: *"Blessed are you when they revile and persecute you, and say all kinds of evil against you falsely for My sake. Rejoice, and be exceedingly glad, for great is your reward in heaven."*

Verse 16 in that same chapter nails it very well: *"Let your light so shine before men, that they may see your good works, and glorify your Father in heaven."* Could it be that God allows these difficult times to come into our lives so that we can be a light and witness for Him to the world? Even the heathen love those who love them, but it takes real character and the supernatural love of Christ to show compassion to our enemies, and those who deliberately hurt us.

God says He is our Vindicator, and vengeance is His, not ours. Romans 12:17-19 makes this clear: *"Repay no one evil for evil. Have regard for good things in the sight of all men. If it is possible, as much as depends on you, live peaceably with all men. Beloved, do not avenge yourselves, but rather give place to wrath; for it is written, "Vengeance is Mine, I will repay, says the Lord."* Verse 21 summarizes the whole matter: *"Do not be overcome by evil, but overcome evil with good."*

1 Peter 5:7 also reminds us: *"Therefore, humble yourselves under the mighty hand of God, that He may exalt you in due time, casting all your care upon Him, for He cares for you."* This is just another area of our Christian walk where we need to exercise faith, trusting God with our relationship problems by truly casting our burdens on Him and trusting Him to help us work things out.

Although it has been a challenge with me, I've found that to be obedient to God and to be a true believer, I must have compassion and tolerance for others. As Christians, we must forgive each offence as it comes, always continuing to walk in the supernatural love of Christ. If we realize the nature of God versus the nature of evil, it's easy to understand why "love your neighbor as yourself" is the second greatest commandment in the Bible. The evil in the world brings suffering, strife, wars and tragedy to people every day. Evil plants discord in homes, families, ministries and churches. Left to itself, evil would quickly destroy and devour the world and all the people in it. But God sent His Son, Jesus, to save us from destruction and eternal death. Through Jesus' crucifixion and resurrection, the power of the devil has been broken for those who choose Christ.

God needs us to be able to work peaceably together, taking His Gospel message into the world. His last words were of great importance, and we should carefully heed them. Just before His departure into heaven, Jesus said in Mark 16:15: *"Go into all the world and preach the Gospel to every creature."* We are the vehicle that God has chosen to use; we are truly His hands and feet. He can only work through His people and through the power of the Holy Spirit to bring His message of hope and redemption to a lost world.

As long as we can work together, bringing truth and light to the world, we will be effective witnesses for Christ; but if our own relationships crumble and fall, so will our testimony. Love is the driving force of Christianity and should be our main focus. The world outside is looking at Christians, searching for something better, something more meaningful, something richer and fuller than they currently have. If people who don't know the Lord's grace see people in the church backbiting, slandering, fighting and devouring one another, it will leave them with the bitter taste of disappointment in their mouths.

What a difference the church could make by embracing an unloved world with the love of Christ! Hurting people need love more than anything else. It is up to the church to demonstrate the love of Jesus Christ. Love is the most powerful tool that we have at our disposal.

Anyone who has God's love burning within holds the power to touch another person's life in a very special way. God needs His people to impart His healing love to the hurting people around them, simply by sharing the burden of their pain and showing compassion. I felt that kind of deep love from God extended to me through my dear friend Sally, when I was at a low point in life. In the same way, simple acts of kindness extended by us to others cover those people with the gentle, healing balm of hope and restoration. It gives them the strength and courage to press forward through difficult times. Our kindness could also hold the power to change eternal destinies.

Love softens the heart. Even the hardest of hearts can't deny the power of love. After years of disappointments and hardships, many people hide their deep pain behind the forbidding walls of a hardened heart. After that wall is built, often the lifestyle becomes rough and menacing as well. Although there are rough and tough girls out there, we see this much more often in men. After years of carrying this tough-guy persona, a man will have himself and everyone around him believing this is the real person, not merely a mask. People tend to shrink back from the tough-guy types and are quick to write them off, deeming them unreachable.

Through personal experience, I have found that true love is a powerful force that can break even the hardest walls surrounding a wounded heart. At the core of every man or woman, no matter how tough, there's still a child who needs something or someone to fill the empty parts of his or her heart. The most powerful way to touch and fill that emptiness is through love, not giving a sermon, not passing judgment, but simply offering love. Love always sees beyond the hard outer shell into a heart that's been broken and deeply wounded.

So love is truly a trait of the Savior. It is the one thing that is capable of bringing healing and tenderness to the hearts of all people. It is the most powerful force in the world and has been changing the hearts of many since the beginning of time. That's why it's so important to God that His people walk in love. Without it, we won't accomplish anything for the Kingdom of God.

All of us rub shoulders with other people every day. These are the people God has put into our lives so that we can touch their hearts and pour out His love on them. This process of changing lives is a very important part of the Gospel message, maybe the most important part. So, as Christians, we need to go out each day into the world in which we live, being watchful and ready to pour out the love of God to the people who need it most.

> *"By this all will know that you are My disciples, if you have love for one another"* (John 13:35).

SECTION SIX

Vision for Tomorrow

Let us run with endurance the race that is set before us, looking unto Jesus, the author and finisher of our faith…. (Hebrews 12:1b-2a)

CHAPTER 19

New Life and Vision Reborn

After seven years of success with the band, we took a three year break from the music. We had two daughters, Sari and Jessica by then. Those three years passed by quickly and with them came two more daughters, Janelle and Ana Leigh, to join their older sisters. With four beautiful children, our family felt complete, and we were busier than ever before. Those were happy and exciting years. Benji and I found that there's nothing quite like giving life to our babies and building a family.

Looking back, I realize what a blessing it was not to have music on my mind during that time. It would have been much too great a burden. There were too many changes taking place in my life with new babies and the added responsibilities and duties that were often overwhelming. I'm thankful for those years and feel they gave me a chance to 'catch my breath'. Solely being a mother and wife, at home with the girls and my husband, also helped me renew my energy and health, which I desperately needed.

But as time moved on, there came the familiar feelings and longings. There were days when my heart pined away for the music again. As our babies grew, so did my desire to get back into the world of singing, entertainment and ministry. When the girls were a little older, we made several attempts at getting groups together. I was excited with newfound energy, new dreams and visions and threw myself wholeheartedly into pursuing them.

Eventually, with a lot of prayer and hard work and through divine connections, we organized a small group of musicians and started moving forward. Adding more people to the mix, we did some concerts. Within several months we got our feet off the ground. Benji and I and our daughters were happy and elated as once again we got into the full swing of a busy concert schedule. After several years of not writing songs or singing (except soft lullabies to my precious babies or humming while I worked) suddenly the songs began pouring out of me again. I spent long hours sitting at the piano or keyboard singing, composing, praying. The fire in my soul was burning again.

Over the years I've had ongoing struggles with not being able to connect with the music and not really feeling passionate about the songs I sang. Many times I felt as if my emotions were locked up, not able to flow to the world outside. This numbness and lack of feeling bothered me, leaving me feeling disconnected and unsettled. I wanted to be affective in making a difference in the world, but I knew it would be impossible to truly give God's love to others when I couldn't connect with His Spirit myself. As I read and pondered the promises that I found in Acts 2: 17-21 (KJV), I felt the familiar sparks of hope burning inside again. I felt the lure of God's Spirit pulling me in as I meditated on these words in my heart:

> *"And it shall come to pass in the last days, saith God; I will pour out My Spirit upon all flesh: and your sons and your daughters shall prophesy, and your young men shall see visions, and your old men shall*

dream dreams. And on my servants and on my handmaidens I will pour out in those days my Spirit; and they shall prophesy: and I will show wonders in heaven above, and signs in the earth beneath; blood, and fire, and vapor of smoke: the sun shall be turned into darkness, and the moon into blood, before that great and notable day of the Lord come. And it shall come to pass, that whosoever shall call on the name of the Lord shall be saved."

These verses pulled me into their sure promises. I wanted God's Spirit to awaken the passion burning in me. I wanted everything He had to offer. Realizing how imperfect and how completely undone I was, I knew that my life could very well fritter itself away, never becoming any more meaningful or fruitful. Without God's Spirit consuming me, I knew the corruption of my soul would surely keep me from gaining true victory over sin and failure once again.

I also remembered reading in the Gospels that Jesus spoke about the power of the Holy Spirit and of His own constant reliance on that power. Before Jesus began His ministry here on earth, John baptized Him, fully immersing Him in water, as an outward symbol of His dedication and commitment to His Father. After Jesus was baptized, *"Immediately, coming up from the water, He saw the heavens parting, and the Spirit descending upon Him like a dove"* (Mark 1:10).

This was a glorious moment in history. I believe this was possibly the most important moment in Jesus' life, as God imparted His Spirit into His beloved Son. This impartation equipped Jesus with supernatural power, making it possible for Him to fulfill all the plans heaven had for Him. Throughout the New Testament, there are beautiful stories written about Jesus' life and the miracles he performed. I am awed by the power He received through the Spirit of God resting upon Him. Jesus listened to the voice of God, and He reminds us of that in John 5:19b: *"Most assuredly, I say to you, the Son can do nothing of Himself, but what He sees the Father do; for whatever He does, the Son also does in like manner."* Relying fully on God's Spirit to lead Him, Jesus touched many people, performing miracles, signs and wonders. He left a great example for us to follow, and urges us to walk in His footsteps, carrying on His ministry until the end of the age.

When Jesus was crucified and buried in the tomb, the power of His blood overcame the power of death, and He rose from the grave, alive forevermore. After a happy and joyous reunion with His disciples, Jesus told them that He would be leaving, that He would ascend into heaven. Naturally, the disciples were sad.

He comforted them in John 14:26: *"But the Helper, the Holy Spirit, whom the Father will send in My name, He will teach you all things, and bring to your remembrance all things that I said to you."* This promise was given for all of humanity down through the ages, including us. Jesus sent His Holy Spirit to dwell among us and within us until we see Him face to face. He said He will not leave us alone or comfortless. What a promise this is! The Bible speaks a great deal about the Holy Spirit leading, guiding and directing us on a very intimate level.

John the Baptist prophesied saying, *"There comes One after me who is mightier than I, whose sandal strap I am not worthy to stoop down and loose. I indeed baptized you with water, but He will baptize you with the Holy Spirit"* (Mark 1:7-8). I believe the single most important thing in our personal Christian walk is to receive the baptism and power of the Holy Spirit. We need to be able to hear the voice of God through His Spirit, so that we can stay in His will. We echo the words of Jesus when He said, *"I can of Myself do nothing. As I hear, I judge; and My judgment is righteous, because I do not seek My own will but the will of the Father who sent Me"* (John 5:30).

I wanted God to reveal Himself to me in a real way. My own humanness and the oppression I felt paled in comparison to the exciting things I was reading about, and I wondered if there was a way for me to walk closer with Him and experience more of His supernatural power in my life. I wanted to experience that power. I wanted to discover the deeper mysteries of His heart and thoughts toward me. Not even really understanding what I was wishing for, I simply knew there was an aching in my soul that had never been satisfied. Remembering that the Bible says in James 4:2b *"You do not have because you do not ask,"* I decided to simply ask the Holy Spirit to fill me, consume me and lead me. I prayed for His power to envelop me, as it did the people in the church of Acts. I asked God to put the fire in my soul and His passion in my heart.

Becoming even more open and vulnerable to Him, I found my prayers coming to pass! The transformation didn't occur suddenly or come with a crashing bolt of thunder or magnificent flash of lightening; no, it silently took place over time, deep within the empty crevices of my soul. Slowly, my inner spirit began to change. Swept up into His presence and calmed by His gentle, yet powerful touch, I felt the deep anxiety, anger and melancholy feelings slipping away. The lonesome feelings of abandonment were replaced with the sure knowledge that Jesus loves me, and will always be there for me. I felt different in a good way.

My husband, Benji, responded to an invitation for prayer after hearing a message on the empowerment that comes with intentionally asking the Holy Spirit to be an active part of every area of our lives. Going forward for prayer, he simply desired to have someone pray with him for a closer connection to God, through His Spirit. As he made his way to the front of the church, God gave him an awesome physical impartation. He felt a sudden surge of tremendous heat go through his body and was instantly drenched from head to toe. Water ran down over his skin and soaked his shirt, as though he'd just walked through a heavy rain. Then just as quickly, his skin was completely dry again. But the warm feeling lingered in his physical body and also in his heart and soul. This was a powerful and riveting experience for him.

I believe God uses extraordinary moments like these to reveal His power to us, mere mortal men and women. Since the Holy Spirit isn't visible to the human eye and cannot be touched, I wonder if physical manifestations such as these are reminders that His power is real and available to everyone who wants to experience it. These moments are exciting and bring hope and a sense of realness to the Christian walk.

Benji and I have enjoyed coming to a better understanding of the mystery of the Godhead: God, Jesus and the Holy Spirit are one God, manifested in three ways. We have been made whole through knowing God as our Father and Creator. Jesus, the Father's Son, came as our Savior and Redeemer. The Holy Spirit is the fulfillment of prophecy as our Comforter and Helper. These three are One Lord.

God speaks to His people many times through the prompting of the Holy Spirit. Among a whole host of other things, the Holy Spirit reminds us to intercede and pray for friends in times of distress. At other times, the Spirit warns us of danger. I thank God every day that I can ask Him to help me make important decisions that will determine my future. In His infinite wisdom, God always knows what is best for us and has provided a way for us to walk closely with Him and hear His voice.

I also know that the Holy Spirit was sent to bring comfort and to take away pain and suffering. Like the sun's rays suddenly bursting through the clouds on a cold, wintry morning, so is God's love bursting forth in my life. I know that something good is happening to me. Something is coming alive in me, and I realize that I have been rescued by a God who is compassionate and full of mercy.

I've also come to realize there is no end to this revolving relationship we have with our Maker. I believe His eyes are carefully watching those who continue to reach higher, draw closer and ask for more. His resources are inexhaustible, His love is undying and His mercy toward us never-ending. There is no end to the possibilities for our lives, if we pursue Him with tenacity, never letting go of His promises for us.

CHAPTER 20

Pressing On

Walking through each door as it opens, Benji and I are living a life that's expectant. There is a continual desire to see God's power displayed to a lost and dying world. We both feel an urgency to go into all the world and share the message of hope and a better life that's only available through knowing Jesus Christ.

As Christians and ambassadors for Christ, we feel that we have a responsibility to spread the Gospel in any way that we can. We understand that we have been bought with a price. If it weren't for Jesus' death and resurrection, we would be destined to a lifetime of mediocrity and hardship followed by eternity in hell. Because of His great love for us, Jesus Christ chose to suffer in our place, laying down His own life for us and taking dominion over sin and death. This great sacrifice allows us to inherit the right to become victorious people of power. We can confidently claim His promises while fulfilling our destiny through Him.

I know with a certainty that God's love for me is stronger and more powerful than anything else I'll ever encounter. His love has set me free from the slavery and bondage of my past. I am so thankful that I've been delivered from the awful torment of panic attacks and paralyzing fear. If my heavenly

Father had not healed the hurt and pain from my mind and body when I cried out to Him, I don't know what my life might have become. Even though I may glimpse hardships that might yet evolve in the future, mountains to climb and rough waters to cross, I know with confidence that if I keep pressing on with Him, I will always gain the victory. I will even come out stronger on the other side.

Because of God's power and authority in my life I will press on, reaching for the high calling, expecting a life that is satisfying and rewarding. As a Christian, I need to take my positions of influence in this world very seriously, because I am a living example of Jesus to the world. People looking in from the outside will not immediately see and know Jesus and His love. No, at first they will only be able to see and know me. If I yield my heart as I should, others will want to know the One that I serve. They, too, will want the blessings and the peace of mind that I have.

Just as an epidemic spreads quickly because of people coming into contact with someone who is a carrier of a disease, so should God's powerful anointing spread across the world because of the unsaved coming into contact with Christians, who are carriers of His love.

Because of my own experiences, I have a strong desire to see people delivered and set free from emotional trauma. I know and understand how a person can quickly become entangled in a dark web of deception and lies, because I lived in the haze of uncertainty that shrouded my thinking for most of my early life. More importantly, I also realize the clarity of mind and confident sureness that comes with knowing and claiming the truth of God's promises. I know the power of God's healing and deliverance, because I am experiencing it every day. Although many unfortunate things happen in this world, I know that He will always make a way for those who fully commit themselves to Him.

I believe God is not only merciful in bringing healing and restoration after experiencing trauma, but also many times He stands directly in the line of fire for us, protecting us from the fiery darts that come against us daily. Our minds cannot fathom, cannot even begin to realize, how this spiritual war constantly rages against us and what the spiritual realm actually looks like.

In Deuteronomy, God gives us a great example of His ability to dismantle the efforts of the enemy, replacing curses with blessings. We read of the evil plotting of Balak, the king of Moab, against the children of Israel who were settling nearby. The king felt more and more threatened by these desert-dwelling people who had caused the fall of Pharaoh. The fearful thoughts and growing anger smoldering within Balak finally consumed his soul. He became desperate to see the destruction of the Israelites.

In an attempt to protect himself and to disarm the people he so feared, Balak hired Balaam to pronounce a curse on Israel. He thought that by weakening them, he would be empowering himself, bringing an end to all his worries. What the king didn't realize was that God always gets the final word! The everlasting Father, who holds the highest position of power and authority, chose not to heed the evil requests of Balak, but instead turned what was meant to be a curse on Israel into many blessings.

As it was for the children of Israel in that day, so it can be for us today: *"The Lord your God turned the curse into a blessing for you, because the Lord your God loved you"* (Deuteronomy 23:5). I believe He continues to protect and renew the lives of those who diligently serve Him, replacing intended curses with blessings. This is the kind of loving and merciful God we serve. This is what He does for His children.

I see no reason to hold on to feelings of disappointment or resentment because of a less than perfect childhood, although

I have struggled terribly with those emotions at times throughout my life. But now, seeing no possible way to change the past, there is only one thing I can do; I can press on into a better future. I have put my trust in the One who gives *"Beauty for ashes, the oil of joy for mourning, the garment of praise for the spirit of heaviness"* (Isaiah 61:3a).

There will always be evil in the world. Many are those who have been snagged by its cruel fingers, who are marked with the scars it has given, and who have borne the heavy burden of its weight. No matter what happens, we can confidently go on to claim the promises found in the Word of God. I find great comfort in Romans 8:28: *"...All things work together for good to those who love God, to those who are called according to His purpose."*

Because of the trauma in my past, I can relate with others who are caught up in the same situations. I can identify with those whose hearts are anguished and broken because of the drastic effects of abuse in their lives. I know how much abuse hurts, emotionally and physically. I know the feelings of hopelessness that follow victims. I know the confusion that wreaks havoc on their minds. Most of all, I know there's hope for a better tomorrow, hope for each curse to be turned into a blessing, and hope for wholeness and healing.

We all have a choice to make. Thank God that we have a choice! Regardless of the past, it's entirely up to us whether we'll choose a future of life or death. God says in Deuteronomy 30:19b-20a:

> *"...I have set before you life and death, blessing and cursing; therefore CHOOSE LIFE, that both you and your descendants may live; that you may love the Lord your God, that you may obey His voice, and that you may cling to Him, for He is your life and the length of your days."*

God's extreme power is always there. His power is never diminished or defeated. He holds the power to give us restoration and a new life in Him. Jesus Christ longs to make His strength known to us, because we are His beloved children:

> *"For the eyes of the Lord run to and fro throughout the whole earth, to show Himself strong on behalf of those whose heart is loyal to Him" (2 Chronicles 16:9a).*

So it's up to each one of us to decide what we'll do with the life that has been given us. The unfortunate things can either strengthen us or tear us down. We can choose to allow those things to destroy us little by little, day by day, or we can choose to let God help us turn our curses into blessings. The choice is completely up to us.

I choose life, a life filled with God and His goodness. Because of His constant presence in my life, I know that my future will be rich and rewarding. I know that I will reap a harvest of good things. Thankfully, now I know the things that were intended to destroy my life have been turned around and will end up being a blessing to me and to others.

I want to share the life God has given me by reaching out to those who are hurting. There's a whole world of hurting people out there: babies to hold, children to love, the hungry to feed and many wounded hearts that need the healing power of God's love. My goal is to carry that love to as many people as I possibly can.

Just as Paul stated in Philippians 3:13-14 (KJV), so do I declare today: *"Brethren, I count not myself to have apprehended: but this one thing I do, forgetting those things which are behind, and reaching forth unto those things which are before, I press toward the mark for the prize of the high calling of God in Christ Jesus."*

I believe there comes the time in everyone's life when we need to leave the past behind, pick ourselves up by the boot straps, and press forward. That time has come for me, and I'm not looking back.

SECTION SEVEN

God's Promises For You

"For as the rain comes down, and the snow from heaven, and do not return there, but water the earth, and make it bring forth and bud, that it may give seed to the sower and bread to the eater, so shall My Word be that goes forth from My mouth, it shall not return to Me void, but it shall accomplish what I please, and it shall prosper in the thing for which I sent it" (Isaiah 55:10-11).

God's Promises for Deliverance from Sin

For You have delivered my soul from death, my eyes from tears, and my feet from falling. (Psalms 116:8)

Bring my soul out of prison that I may praise Your name; the righteous shall surround me, for You shall deal bountifully with me. (Psalms 142:7)

The Lord is near to all who call upon Him, to all who call on Him in truth. He will fulfill the desire of those who fear Him; He also will hear their cry, and save them. (Psalms 145:18-19)

...When the enemy comes in like a flood, the Spirit of the Lord will lift up a standard against Him. (Isaiah 59:19b)

"I will give you a new heart and will put a new spirit within you; I will take the heart of stone out of your flesh and give you a heart of flesh. I will put My Spirit within you and cause you to walk in My statutes, and you will keep my judgments and do them." (Ezekiel 36:26-27)

"However, when He, the Spirit of Truth has come, He will guide you into all truth.,,." (John 16:13a)

"...God, having raised up His Servant Jesus, sent Him to bless you, in turning away every one of you from your iniquities." (Acts 3:26)

Therefore "Come out from among them, and be separate, says the Lord. Do not touch what is unclean and I will receive you. I will be a Father to you, and you shall be My sons and daughters, says the Lord Almighty." (2 Corinthians 6:17-18)

Giving thanks to the Father who has qualified us to be partakers of the inheritance of the saints in light. He has delivered us from the power of darkness and conveyed us into the kingdom of the Son of His love, in whom we have redemption through His blood, the forgiveness of sins. (Colossians 1:12-14)

Let us therefore come boldly to the throne of grace, that we may obtain mercy and find grace to help in time of need. (Hebrews 4:16)

For this purpose, the Son of God was manifested, that He might destroy the works of the devil. (1 John 3:8b)

You are of God, little children, and have overcome them, because He who is in you is greater than he who is in the world. (1 John 4:4)

God's Promises for a New Life in Christ

He restores my soul; He leads me in the paths of righteousness for His name's sake. (Psalms 23:3)

Bless the Lord, O my soul, and forget not all His benefits: who forgives all your iniquities, who heals all your diseases, who redeems your life from destruction, who crowns you with lovingkindness and tender mercies, who satisfies your mouth with good things, so that your youth is renewed like the eagle's. (Psalms 103:2-5)

The Lord will perfect that which concerns me; Your mercy, O Lord, endures forever; do not forsake the works of Your hands. (Psalms 138:8)

Do not remember the former things, nor consider the things of old. Behold, I will do a new thing, now it shall spring forth, shall you not know it? I will even make a road in the wilderness and rivers in the desert. (Isaiah 43:18-19)

I will restore to you the years that the swarming locust has eaten.... (Joel 2:25a)

"Come to Me, all you who labor and are heavy laden, and I will give you rest. Take my yoke upon you and learn from Me, for I am gentle and lowly in heart, and you will find rest for your souls. For My yoke is easy and My burden is light." (Matthew 11:28-30)

"I have come that they may have life, and that they may have it more abundantly." (John 10:10b)

...Just as Christ was raised from the dead by the glory of the Father, even so we also should walk in newness of life. (Romans 6:4b)

And do not be conformed to this world, but be transformed by the renewing of your mind, that you may prove what is that good and acceptable and perfect will of God. (Romans 12:2)

Therefore, if anyone is in Christ, he is a new creation; old things have passed away; behold, all things have become new. (2 Corinthians 5:17)

For we are His workmanship created in Christ Jesus for good works, which God prepared beforehand, that we should walk in them. (Ephesians 2:10)

Now to Him who is able to do exceedingly abundantly above all that we ask or think, according to the power that works in us, to Him be glory in the church by Christ Jesus to all generations, forever and ever. (Ephesians 3:20-21)

Being confident of this very thing, that He who has begun a good work in you will complete it until the day of Jesus Christ. (Philippians 1:6)

God's Promises for Overcoming the Spirit of Fear

Be strong and of good courage, do not fear, nor be afraid of them; for the Lord your God, He is the One who goes with you. He will not leave you nor forsake you. (Deuteronomy 31:6)

The Lord, He is the One who goes before you. He will be with you, He will not leave you nor forsake you; do not fear nor be dismayed. (Deuteronomy 31:8)

"...As I was with Moses, so I will be with you. I will not leave you nor forsake you." (Joshua 1:5b)

The Lord also will be a refuge for the oppressed, a refuge in times of trouble. And those who know Your name will put their trust in You; for You, Lord, have not forsaken those who seek You. (Psalms 9: 9-10)

Yea, though I walk through the valley of the shadow of death, I will fear no evil; for You are with me; Your rod and Your staff, they comfort me. (Psalms 23:4)

The Lord is my light and my salvation; whom shall I fear? The Lord is the strength of my life; of whom shall I be afraid? (Psalms 27:1)

God is our refuge and strength, a very present help in trouble. (Psalms 46:1)

Whenever I am afraid, I will trust in You. In God I will praise His Word, in God I have put my trust.... (Psalms 56:3-4)

He who dwells in the secret place of the Most high shall abide under the shadow of the Almighty. I will say of the Lord, "He is my refuge and my fortress, my God, in Him will I trust." (Psalms 91:1-2)

No evil shall befall you, nor shall any plague come near your dwelling; for He shall give His angels charge over you, to keep you in all your ways. (Psalms 91:10-11)

The Lord is on my side; I will not fear. What can man do to me? (Psalms 118:6)

"Fear not, for I am with you; be not dismayed, for I am your God. I will strengthen you, yes, I will help you, I will uphold you with My righteous right hand." (Isaiah 41:10)

"...Fear not, for I have redeemed you; I have called you by name; You are mine." (Isaiah 43:1b)

"Peace I leave with you. My peace I give to you; not as the world gives do I give to you. Let not your heart be troubled, neither let it be afraid." (John 14:27)

For God has not given us a spirit of fear, but of power and of love and of a sound mind. (2 Timothy 1:7)

God's Promises for Becoming a True Believer

I will instruct you and teach you in the way which you shall go; I will guide you with My eye. (Psalms 32:8)

The steps of a good man are ordered by the Lord, and He delights in his way. Though he fall he shall not be utterly cast down; for the Lord upholds him with His hand. (Psalms 37:23-24)

Because he has set his love upon Me, therefore will I deliver him; I will set him on high, because he hath known My name. He shall call upon Me, and I will answer him; I will be with him in trouble; I will deliver him and honor him. (Psalms 91:14-15)

Commit your works to the Lord, and your thoughts will be established. (Proverbs 16:3)

He who covers his sins will not prosper, but whoever confesses and forsakes them will have mercy. (Proverbs 28:13)

Let the wicked forsake his way, and the unrighteous man his thoughts; let him return to the Lord, and He will have mercy upon Him; and to our God, for He will abundantly pardon. (Isaiah 55:7)

"You will seek Me and find Me, when you search for Me with all your heart. I will be found by you, says the Lord." (Jeremiah 29:13-14a)

Yet in all these things we are more than conquerors through Him who loved us. (Romans 8:37)

The Word is near you, in your mouth and in your heart, that if you confess with your mouth the Lord Jesus and believe in your heart that God has raised Him from the dead, you will be saved. For with the heart one believes unto righteousness, and with the mouth confession is made unto salvation. (Romans 10:8b-10)

So then faith comes by hearing, and hearing by the Word of God. (Romans 10:17)

"...My grace is sufficient for you; for My strength is made perfect in weakness." (2 Corinthians 12:9a)

Finally, brethren, whatever things are true, whatever things are noble, whatever things are just, whatever things are pure, whatever things are lovely, whatever things are of good report, if there is any virtue and if there is anything praiseworthy—meditate on these things. The things which you have learned and received and heard and saw in me, these do, and the God of peace will be with you. (Philippians 4:8-9)

Now faith is the substance of things hoped for, the evidence of things not seen. (Hebrews 11:1)

He is a rewarder of those who diligently seek Him. (Hebrews 11:6b)

If we confess our sins, He is faithful and just to forgive us our sins and to cleanse us from all unrighteousness. (1 John 1:9)

God's Promises for the Empowerment of the Holy Spirit

The Spirit of God has made me, and the breath of the Almighty gives me life. (Job 33:4)

"I will put My Spirit within you, and cause you to walk in My statutes, and you will keep My judgments and do them." (Ezekiel 36:27)

"...There comes One after Me who is mightier than I, whose sandal strap I am not worthy to stoop down and loose. I indeed baptized you with water, but He will baptize you with the Holy Spirit." (Mark 1:7-8)

"If you then, being evil, know how to give good gifts to your children, how much more will your heavenly Father give the Holy Spirit to those who ask Him!" (Luke 11:13)

"But the Helper, the Holy Spirit, whom the Father will send in My name, He will teach you all things, and bring to your remembrance all things that I said to you." (John 14:26)

"Abide in Me, and I in you. As the branch cannot bear fruit of itself, unless it abides in the vine, neither can you, unless you abide in Me. I am the vine, you are the branches. He who abides in Me, and I in him, bears much fruit; for without Me you can do nothing." (John 15:4-5)

"You shall receive power when the Holy Spirit has come upon you: and you shall be witnesses to me in Jerusalem, and in all Judea and Samaria, and to the end of the earth." (Acts 1:8)

There is therefore now no condemnation to those who are in Christ Jesus, who do not walk according to the flesh, but according to the Spirit. (Romans 8:1)

For as many as are led by the Spirit of God, these are sons of God. (Romans 8:14)

Now may the God of all hope fill you with all joy and peace in believing, that you may abound in hope by the power of the Holy Spirit. (Romans 15:13)

Now we have received, not the spirit of the world, but the Spirit who is from God, that we might know the things that have been freely given to us by God. These things we also speak, not in words which man's wisdom teaches, but which the Holy Spirit teaches... (1 Corinthians 2:12-13a)

Do you not know that your body is the temple of the Holy Spirit who is in you, whom you have from God, and you are not your own? (1 Corinthians 6:19)

The fruit of the Spirit is love, joy, peace, longsuffering, kindness, goodness, faithfulness, gentleness, self-control. Against such there is no law. And those who are Christ's have crucified the flesh with its passions and desires. If we live in the Spirit, let us also walk in the Spirit. (Galatians 5: 22-25)

God's Promises for Spiritual and Physical Healing

The Lord is near to those who have a broken heart, and saves such as have a contrite spirit. (Psalms 34:18)

Trust in the Lord with all your heart, and lean not on your own understanding; in all your ways acknowledge Him, and He shall direct your paths. Do not be wise in your own eyes; fear the Lord and depart from evil. It will be health to your flesh, and strength to your bones. (Proverbs 3:5-8)

...Give attention to My words; incline your ear to My sayings. Do not let them depart from your eyes; keep them in the midst of your heart; for they are life to those who find them, and health to all their flesh. (Proverbs 4:20-22)

That He would grant you, according to the riches of His glory, to be strengthened with might through His Spirit in the inner man. (Ephesians 3:16)

Now may the God of peace Himself sanctify you completely; and may your whole spirit, soul and body be preserved blameless at the coming of our Lord Jesus Christ. (1 Thessalonians 5:23)

Who Himself bore our sins in His own body on the tree, that we, having died to sins, might live for righteousness—by whose stripes you were healed. (1 Peter 2:24)

God's Promises for a Blessed Future

The Lord bless you and keep you; the Lord make His face to shine upon you, and be gracious to you; the Lord lift up His countenance upon you, and give you peace. (Numbers 6:24-26)

The Lord your God turned the curse into a blessing for you, because the Lord your God loves you. (Deuteronomy 23:5b)

I have set before you life and death, blessing and cursing; therefore choose life, that both you and your descendants may live; that you may love the Lord your God, that you may obey His voice, and that you may cling to Him, for He is your life and the length of your days.... (Deuteronomy 30:19b-20)

For the eyes of the Lord run to and fro throughout the whole earth, to show Himself strong on behalf of those whose heart is loyal to Him. (2 Chronicles 16:9a)

You will show me the path of life; in Your presence is fullness of joy; at Your right hand are pleasures forevermore. (Psalms 16:11)

Surely goodness and mercy shall follow me all the days of my life; and I will dwell in the house of the Lord forever. (Psalms 23:6)

Trust in the Lord with all your heart, and lean not on your own understanding; in all your ways acknowledge Him, and He shall direct your paths. (Proverbs 3:5-6)

Those who wait on the Lord shall renew their strength; they shall mount up with wings like eagles, they shall run and not be weary, they shall walk and not faint. (Isaiah 40: 31)

"For I know the plans I have for you," declares the Lord, "plans to prosper you and not to harm you, plans to give you a hope and a future." (Jeremiah 29:11 NIV)

If you extend your soul to the hungry and satisfy the afflicted soul, then your light shall dawn in the darkness, and your darkness shall be as the noonday. The Lord will guide you continually, and satisfy your soul in drought, and strengthen your bones; you shall be like a watered garden, and like a spring of water, whose waters do not fail. (Isaiah 58:10-11)

And we know that all things work together for good to those who love God, to those who are called according to His purpose. (Romans 8:28)

...As it is written: "Eye has not seen, nor ear heard, nor have entered into the heart of man the things which God has prepared for those who love Him." (1 Corinthians 2:9)

Therefore we do not lose heart. Even though the outward man is perishing, yet the inward man is being renewed day by day. For our light affliction, which is but for a moment, is working for us a far more exceeding and eternal weight of glory. (2 Corinthians 4:16-17)

And my God shall supply all your need according to His riches in glory by Christ Jesus. (Philippians 4:19)

Let us lay aside every weight, and the sin which so easily ensnares us, and let us run with endurance the race that is set before us, looking unto Jesus, the author and finisher of our faith, who for the joy that was set before Him endured the cross, despising the shame, and has sat down at the right hand of the throne of God. (Hebrews 12:1b-2)